ARTIFICIAL INTELLIGENCE

MIRRORS FOR THE MIND

Harry Henderson

CHELSEA HOUSE
PUBLISHERS
An imprint of Infobase Publishing

To the researchers, the visionaries, and the critics.

Chelsea House
An imprint of Infobase Publishing
132 West 31st Street
New York NY 10001

ISBN-10: 0-8160-5749-4
ISBN-13: 978-0-8160-5749-8

Library of Congress Cataloging-in-Publication Data

Henderson, Harry.
    Artificial intelligence : mirrors for the mind / Harry Henderson.
        p. cm. — (Milestones in discovery and invention)
    Includes bibliographical references and index.
ISBN 0-8160-5749-4
1. Artificial intelligence. I. Title. II. Series.
    Q335.H455 2007
    006.3.—dc22   2006016639

Chelsea House books are available at special discounts when purchased in bulk quantities for businesses, associations, institutions, or sales promotions. Please call our Special Sales Department in New York at (212) 967-8800 or (800) 322-8755.

You can find Chelsea House on the World Wide Web at http://www.chelseahouse.com

Text design by James Scotto-Lavino
Cover design by Dorothy M. Preston
Illustrations by Sholto Ainslie and Melissa Ericksen

Printed in the United States of America

MP FOF 10 9 8 7 6 5 4 3 2 1

This book is printed on acid-free paper.

CONTENTS

PREFACE

The Milestones in Discovery and Invention set is based on a simple but powerful idea—that science and technology are not separate from people's daily lives. Rather, they are part of seeking to understand and reshape the world, an activity that virtually defines being human.

More than a million years ago, the ancestors of modern humans began to shape stones into tools that helped them compete with the specialized predators around them. Starting about 35,000 years ago, the modern type of human, *Homo sapiens*, also created elaborate cave paintings and finely crafted art objects, showing that technology had been joined with imagination and language to compose a new and vibrant world of culture. Humans were not only shaping their world but representing it in art and thinking about its nature and meaning.

Technology is a basic part of that culture. The mythologies of many peoples include a trickster figure, who upsets the settled order of things and brings forth new creative and destructive possibilities. In many myths, for instance, a trickster such as the Native Americans' Coyote or Raven steals fire from the gods and gives it to human beings. All technology, whether it harnesses fire, electricity, or the energy locked in the heart of atoms or genes, partakes of the double-edged gift of the trickster, providing power to both hurt and heal.

An inventor of technology is often inspired by the discoveries of scientists. Science as we know it today is younger than technology, dating back about 500 years to a period called the Renaissance. During the Renaissance, artists and thinkers began to explore nature systematically, and the first modern scientists, such as Leonardo da Vinci (1452–1519) and Galileo Galilei (1564–1642), used instruments and experiments to develop and test ideas about how objects in the universe behaved. A succession of revolutions followed, often introduced by individual geniuses: Isaac Newton (1643–1727) in mechanics and mathematics, Charles Darwin (1809–1882) in biological evolution, Albert Einstein (1879–1955) in relativity and quantum physics, James Watson (1928–   ) and Francis Crick (1916–2004) in modern genetics. Today's emerging fields of science and technology, such as genetic engineering, nanotechnology, and artificial intelligence, have their own inspiring leaders.

The fact that particular names such as Newton, Darwin, and Einstein can be so easily associated with these revolutions suggests the importance of the individual in modern science and technology. Each book in this set thus focuses on the lives and achievements of eight to 10 individuals who together have revolutionized an aspect of science or technology. Each book presents a different field: marine science, genetics, astronomy and space science, forensic science, communications technology, robotics, artificial intelligence, and mathematical simulation. Although early pioneers are included where appropriate, the emphasis is generally on researchers who worked in the 20th century or are still working today.

The biographies in each volume are placed in an order that reflects the flow of the individuals' major achievements, but these life stories are often intertwined. The achievements of particular men and women cannot be understood without some knowledge of the times they lived in, the people they worked with, and developments that preceded their research. Newton famously remarked, "If I have seen further [than others], it is by standing on the shoulders of giants." Each scientist or inventor builds upon—or wrestles with—the work that has come before. Individual scientists and inventors also interact with others in their own laboratories and elsewhere, sometimes even partaking in vast collective efforts, such as the government and private projects that raced at the end of the 20th century to complete the description of the human genome. Scientists and inventors affect, and are affected by, economic, political, and social forces as well. The relationship between scientific and technical creativity and developments in social institutions is another important facet of this series.

A number of additional features provide further context for the biographies in these books. Each chapter includes a chronology and suggestions for further reading. In addition, a glossary and a general bibliography (including organizations and Web resources) appear at the end of each book. Several types of sidebars are also used in the text to explore particular aspects of the profiled scientists' and inventors' work:

Connections Describes the relationship between the featured work and other scientific or technical developments.

I Was There Presents first-hand accounts of discoveries or inventions.

Issues Discusses scientific or ethical issues raised by the discovery or invention.

Other Scientists (or Inventors) Describes other individuals who played an important part in the work being discussed.

Parallels Shows parallel or related discoveries.

Social Impact Suggests how the discovery or invention affects or might affect society and daily life.

Solving Problems Explains how a scientist or inventor dealt with a particular technical problem or challenge.

Trends Presents data or statistics showing how developments in a field changed over time.

Our hope is that readers will be intrigued and inspired by these stories of the human quest for understanding, exploration, and innovation. We have tried to provide the context and tools to enable readers to forge their own connections and to further pursue their fields of interest.

ACKNOWLEDGMENTS

I would like to acknowledge the researchers and staff who helped me obtain photographs of the artificial intelligence pioneers featured in this book, as well as of their work. I would also like to express my continuing appreciation for the ongoing help of Frank K. Darmstadt, my editor.

INTRODUCTION

"**A**rtificial Intelligence." Just putting the two words together is like issuing a challenge. When the chart of the animal kingdom was first laid out by naturalists, humans reserved for themselves the exalted name *Homo sapiens*. The ancient Greeks saw the rational faculties as distinguishing humans from other creatures. Many religious thinkers added to this the notion of the soul, a permanent and essential identity infused into people by their divine creator.

The birth of modern science in the 17th and 18th centuries and the work of thinkers such as René Descartes, Isaac Newton, and Gottfried Leibniz brought a new question into play. If the Universe was really a sort of huge, complex machine subject only to the laws of nature, then perhaps people, too, were really machines. But what was the role of the mind in the human machine? This question arose naturally from dualism, or the split between mind on the one hand and body on the other. The brain was part of the body, but how was it connected to the structures of thought, perception, and imagination?

As the 20th century progressed many new views and explanations would be heard. Alan Turing, the first person profiled in this volume, developed a mathematical proof that said that some kinds of problems could not be solved through computation. On the other hand, all possible computations can be done by a hypothetical machine, a "universal computer." When actual computing machines came along in the 1940s, Turing went on to ask key questions that would continue to preoccupy artificial intelligence (AI) researchers for almost six decades and counting: Can what the mind does be expressed as computation? Can a computer be so advanced people cannot tell that it *is* a computer? Before his tragically early death,

Turing predicted that by the end of the century people would find the idea of intelligent computers to be at least plausible.

The first generation of electronic digital computers grew steadily in power, and the 1950s saw the establishment of AI as a distinct field of research. One of the pioneers in this volume, John McCarthy, coined the term *artificial intelligence* and organized the 1956 conference at Dartmouth that displayed the field's first fruits and suggested its future agenda. Two other featured AI researchers, Allen Newell and Herbert Simon, created programs that could apply the rules of logic, form hypotheses, and solve problems—all things that most people would consider to be signs of intelligence.

Meanwhile, the course of AI research had split into two currents. Researchers such as McCarthy, Newell, and Simon focused on programming logical structures and ways to manipulate symbols and understand language. They focused on computation. The other current, found in early work with neural networks, suggested that the road to AI was to be found in creating complex webs of connections similar to those found in the neurons in the brain, and to develop simple but powerful ways of reinforcing such connections. This would allow the network to learn how, for example, to recognize a letter or a shape. Another featured scientist, Marvin Minsky, developed these ideas and added a new theory of the mind—that it consisted of many layers of different "agents" that dealt with different aspects of knowledge and cooperated as a "society of mind" from which our intelligence and consciousness emerged.

By the 1970s, considerable progress had been made in both of these currents of AI. However, the hoped-for breakthrough to a general-purpose artificial intelligence that could understand natural human language and deal with a wide variety of problems still seemed rather far away. The next two featured researchers, Edward Feigenbaum and Douglas Lenat, shared with many earlier colleagues a belief that a major obstacle to versatile AI was that computer programs lacked common sense. That is, they did not have the broad base of knowledge about how the world works that a human six year old already possesses.

Marvin Minsky had begun to address this lack through the development of frames, or structured descriptions of facts or situations in daily life. Feigenbaum developed a way to create a "knowledge base" of assertions about a particular field of expertise, and a program called an "inference engine" that could search the knowledge base for applicable rules and logically construct an answer to the user's question. By the end of the 1980s "expert systems" using these techniques were doing everything from diagnosing infectious diseases and car trouble to figuring out the best way for an airline to deploy its planes efficiently. Meanwhile, Douglas Lenat has embarked on a decades-long project called Cyc (short for encyclopedia) that continues to this day, compiling millions of facts and relationships and developing sophisticated tools to deal with them.

Historically AI researchers have tended to make bold, confident predictions that such goals as language understanding, robust problem solving, and commonsense reasoning would be achieved in a matter of only a few years. Actual progress has always been much slower. After all, there is not even a single widely accepted theory about what intelligence actually consists of. Nevertheless, AI research and the related field of cognitive science—the study of thinking in brain and machine—have shed much light on each other's concerns. To the extent researchers learn about the brain, they can create computer simulations that seek to capture its processing. To the extent they try out new ideas about cognition with computers, they might learn more about the brain in turn.

The AI field has also been the subject of vigorous (and often heated) debate. This volume features three final people who bring quite different perspectives to the field. Joseph Weizenbaum created a deceptively simple program called ELIZA in the mid-1960s. The program echoed back the user's statements in a way similar to that of certain modern psychotherapists. Alarmed at how readily people confided in the machine, Weizenbaum undertook a critique of the use and misuse of computer power. He suggested that people both overestimated the prowess of the machines and misused them to serve military and other purposes contrary to humane values.

Philosopher Hubert Dreyfus also criticized the use of computers, but his major critique involved his assertion that the human mind is not like a computer at all. The brain is part of a body, and the body is deeply and intricately connected to the living environment. As a follower of "phenomenological" philosophy, Dreyfus has attempted with only partial success to carry on a dialogue or dispute with AI researchers over the years.

Finally, the volume ends with the ultimate question: is a true artificial intelligence possible—and if it is, what will it do to us flesh-and-blood humans? This question has been addressed head-on by our last subject (and one of our most interesting), Ray Kurzweil. A prolific inventor who brought the world a reading machine for the blind, scanners, and music synthesizers, Kurzweil has focused in recent years on trying to answer the big questions about AI. His answer is that the explosive growth of computing power and the ability to scan the brain with greater and greater resolution will, in a few decades, lead to AI that equals and then surpasses human capabilities. People will also be able to enhance their capabilities using this technology. Response to Kurzweil has ranged from exhilaration to dismay at the possibility of technology getting out of control and perhaps resulting in the extinction of the human species.

Wherever the future may lead, the history of AI and the people who made it are fascinating. Their work continues to shape many of the products in use today, from navigation systems to online financial planning tools. In the end, though, AI is most fascinating because it asks us how much we understand about ourselves and challenges us to imagine and perhaps face the nearly unimaginable.

1

BEYOND CALCULATION

ALAN TURING AND THE BIRTH OF
ARTIFICIAL INTELLIGENCE

At the dawn of the computer age Alan Turing's startling range of original thought led to the creation of many branches of computer science ranging from the fundamental theory of computability to the question of what might constitute true artificial intelligence.

Alan Turing was born in London on June 23, 1912. His father worked in the Indian (colonial) Civil Service, while his mother came from a family that had produced a number of distinguished scientists. Because his parents were often away Turing was raised mainly by relatives until he was of school age. As quoted in a letter in Andrew Hodges's biography of Turing, the boy's nanny noted that

> *The thing that stands out most in my mind was his integrity and his intelligence for a child so young as he then was, also you couldn't camouflage anything from him. I remember one day Alan and I playing together. I played so that he should win, but he spotted it. There was commotion for a few minutes . . .*

Science and Friendship

Young Turing then went as a boarding student to various private schools, finally attending Sherborne School, a college preparatory

Alan Turing developed a theory of computation, oversaw the birth of the computer, and then asked some big questions about the future of machine intelligence. (Photo Researchers)

school. As a youth Turing showed great interest and aptitude in both chemistry and mathematics, although his work was criticized for sloppiness and he tended to neglect other subjects (ignoring Greek completely). As quoted by Hodges, one of Turing's math teachers further observed that the boy "spends a good deal of time apparently in investigations of advanced mathematics to the neglect of elementary work."

Turing suffered from the arbitrary discipline and hazing characteristic of the schools of the time, which emphasized athletics and "school spirit" and suppressed signs of individuality. Hodges notes that Turing's pervasive sense of loneliness was finally pierced when he met an older student, Christopher Morcom, with whom he was able to share his intense interest in mathematics and physics. Turing had not been told, however, that Morcom had contracted tuberculosis, and his sudden death in 1930 was devastating, though it brought the Turing and Morcom families closer together. When Morcom's father established a science prize in his son's honor, Turing won it the first year for a deep mathematical study of a seemingly simple iodine reaction.

In his last years at Sherborne, Turing's mind was absorbed by Einstein's theory of relativity and the new field of quantum mechanics, subjects that few of the most advanced scientific minds of the time could grasp. Turing seemed to recognize instinctively how they represented what today would be called "thinking outside the box." (One of the books Turing received as part of his Morcom Prize was

Mathematical Basis of Quantum Mechanics by future computer pioneer John von Neumann.)

Does It Compute?

Turing's uneven academic performance made it difficult for him to proceed to university, but in 1930 he won a scholarship to King's College of Cambridge University. Turing had begun to apply himself more systematically to the task of becoming a mathematician. Turing's interest then turned to one of the most perplexing unsolved problems of contemporary mathematics. Kurt Gödel had devised a way of "encoding" or assigning special numbers to mathematical assertions. He had shown that in any system of mathematics there will be some assertions that can be neither proved nor disproved. (This is something like the statement: "This statement cannot be proven." If one could prove it is true, it would be false!)

But another great mathematician, David Hilbert, had asked whether there was a way to tell whether any particular mathematical assertion was provable. (Besides its implications for the nature of mathematics itself, this question also had practical consequences in terms of deciding what can be computed.)

Instead of pursuing conventional mathematical strategies to tackle this problem, Turing reimagined the problem by creating the Turing Machine, an abstract "computer" that performs only two kinds of operations: writing or not writing a symbol on its imaginary tape, and possibly moving one space on the tape to the left or right. Turing showed that from this simple set of states and operations any possible type of calculation could be constructed. His 1936 paper "On Computable Numbers" together with Alonzo Church's more traditional logical approach defined the theory of computability.

Because of his use of an imaginary machine, Turing's answer to the computability problem would prove to be quite fortunate. On the one hand, Turing's work demonstrated that not every problem could be solved through computation. On the other hand, because the Turing Machine was universally applicable, it showed that any problem that *could* be computed could in principle be solved through the use of a suitable machine and procedure, or algorithm. In just a few years Turing and other mathematicians and inventors would be designing and implementing digital computers that would turn the potential for computation into reality.

From Symbols to Codes

Turing's mathematical horizons broadened when he had the opportunity to go to the Institute of Advanced Study at Princeton and personally encounter von Neumann, Church, G. H. Hardy, and even

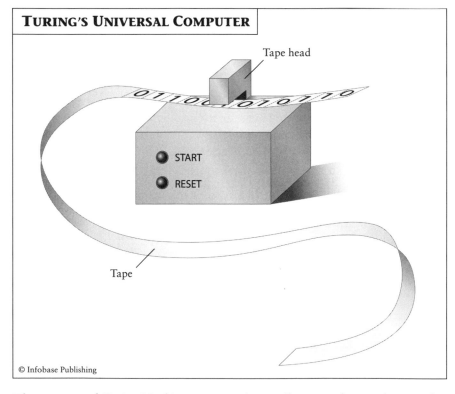

The conceptual Turing Machine consists of an endless tape that can be moved back and forth while recording or erasing symbols.

Albert Einstein. Turing soon plunged into a variety of new projects and ideas. In a letter to his mother, he noted:

> *You have often asked me about possible applications of various branches of mathematics. I have just discovered a possible application of the kind of thing that I am working on at present. It answers the question 'What is the most general kind of code or cipher possible,' and at the same time (rather naturally) enables me to construct a lot of particular and interesting codes.*

After receiving his doctorate from Princeton in 1938, Turing returned to England. In his baggage was a primitive electromechanical computer that he had built. It could multiply two binary numbers.

As Nazi Germany and the Western Allies edged toward war, the importance of code security and codebreaking increased. On September 3, 1939, Germany attacked Poland and Britain and France in turn declared war on Germany. The following day, Turing joined the British government's Code and Cypher School at Bletchley Park, a mansion in a country town where the railway lines connecting London with Oxford and Cambridge met. This secret installation would become the hub for a revolution in computing.

In its simplest form a cipher is a system in which a message (called "plain text") is turned into a coded message (or "cipher text") by substituting a different letter for each letter in the message. Of course such a simple cipher would be easy to guess. By the mid-20th century practical ciphers used more complicated rules or made a repeated series of substitutions, generated by increasingly sophisticated machines.

Riddling the Enigma

The German cipher machine, called Enigma, was a state-of-the-art version of a machine that used multiple wheels or rotors, each of which contained an alphabet. To send a message, the operator first set three (later, four) rotors so that the letters for the day's code showed in a window. The operator also made specified connections on a "plug board" (like an old-fashioned phone switchboard) on the front of the machine. When the operator typed a letter of the original message text, a light indicated the corresponding letter of cipher text. As the rotors moved, they created a continually changing cipher. Between the rotors and the plug board, the machine had trillions of possible settings. The Germans had every reason to believe that their cipher was unbreakable.

Of course codebreakers were trying to keep up with the code-makers. In 1938, the Polish intelligence service came up with an ingenious idea: They wired together a series of Enigma machines

The World War II German Enigma cipher machine used multiple wheels and plugs to create trillions of possible letter combinations. (Photo Researchers)

(which were commercially available) so they would step through the rotor positions and look for key patterns of repeated letters. Because the machine made a ticking sound while it was running, it was nicknamed the "Bombe." However, later that year the Germans changed their system so that the Enigma operator could choose three rotors from a set of five when setting up the machine. With 60 (5 × 4 × 3) possible combinations of rotors, the "Bombe" approach was no longer practical.

Codebreakers would need a more general, programmable machine that could scan for patterns in the Enigma messages. They had to take advantage of the fact that each of the millions of Enigma settings had its own internal consistency. The fact that certain letters were encoded as certain other letters meant that other possible letter matches could not be true.

Fortunately, Turing had already worked out the theory for just such a machine in his paper "On Computable Numbers." Asking whether a number was computable was somewhat like asking whether a given cipher message could match a given original (or "plain text") message, allowing for possible plugboard settings. Using a technique called traffic analysis and looking for patterns, the cipherbreakers could construct a machine that would use Turing's methods to test them against the possibilities.

These methods allowed the British to read German Enigma messages until February 1942, when the Germans added a fourth rotor to the Enigma machine. Turing and his Bletchley Park colleagues responded by creating machines that could rapidly read stored patterns from paper tape. Finally, in 1943, they built Colossus, an early electronic digital computer that could process about 245,000 characters per second!

Turing's wartime work also included a visit to the United States, where he met with scientists and engineers at Bell Labs. One of his most important acquaintances was Claude Shannon, who was developing a groundbreaking theory of communications and information transmission. When they talked, Turing and Shannon found that they were both interested in the idea that a machine could imitate the functions of the human brain. However, one time when Turing was excitedly talking about these ideas in the executive lunchroom, he was heard to say, "No, I'm not interested in developing a *powerful* brain.

All I'm after is a *mediocre* brain, something like the President of the American Telephone and Telegraph Company."

Designing Electronic Computers

As the war drew to an end Turing's imagination brought together what he had seen of the possibilities of automatic computation, and particularly the faster machines that would be made possible by harnessing electronics rather than electromechanical relays. However, there were formidable challenges facing computer designers on both sides of the Atlantic. In particular, how was data to be stored and loaded into the machine? The paper tapes used in Colossus were cumbersome and prone to breakage. Magnetic tape was better but still involved a lot of moving parts. Something akin to the RAM (random access memory) in today's computers was needed. Finally Turing settled on something called an acoustic delay line, a mercury-filled pipe that could circulate sound pulses representing data. (This device was already used to keep radar signals displayed on a screen.) While mainstream computer designers would eventually turn to such technologies as cathode-ray tubes and magnetic "core" memory, Turing's idea was imaginative and practical for the time.

In 1946, after he had moved to the National Physical Laboratory in Teddington, England, Turing received a government grant to build the ACE (Automatic Computing Engine). This machine's design incorporated advanced programming concepts such as the storing of all instructions in the form of programs in memory without the mechanical setup steps required for machines such as the ENIAC. Another important idea of Turing's was that programs could modify themselves by treating their own instructions just like other data in memory. This idea of self-modifying programs (which had been independently arrived at by American John von Neumann and the American ENIAC team) would be a key to developing AI programs that could adapt themselves to different circumstances. However, the engineering of the advanced memory system ran into problem and delays, and Turing left the project in 1948 (it would be completed in 1950).

Toward AI

What ultimately impressed Turing and a handful of other researchers (such as John von Neumann) was not the ability of the new machines to calculate rapidly, but their potential to manipulate symbols. The wartime work had shown how a machine could find and act on patterns. Turing's theoretical work had shown that computers were potentially "universal machines"—any such machine can simulate any other. This brought the enticing possibility that the human brain itself was a machine that could be simulated by an "artificial brain." The symbol-manipulation behavior called intelligence in humans could thus be embodied in artificial intelligence.

Thus, in 1947, Turing wrote a paper titled "Intelligent Machinery" that would remain unpublished for more than 20 years. In this seminal paper, Turing states that the path to creating an intelligent machine is to design a device that is analogous to the human brain in important ways. In particular, the machine must have the capacity to learn as a human infant learns, given suitable teaching methods.

This idea of a machine that can learn as a child learns was far ahead of its time—in the 1990s, it would be the focus of a robotics project at the Massachusetts Institute of Technology under Rodney Brooks. But some first steps could be taken even given the still-primitive computing technology of the 1940s.

A possibility that came immediately to Turing was the game of chess. Playing chess certainly seemed to demonstrate human intelligence. If a computer could play chess well (and especially if it could learn from its mistakes), it would arguably be intelligent. Turing began to develop the outlines of an approach to computer chess. Although he did not finish his program, it demonstrated some relevant algorithms for choosing moves and led to later work by Claude Shannon, Allen Newell, and other researchers—and ultimately to Deep Blue, the computer that defeated world chess champion Garry Kasparov in 1997.

Indeed, although it would not be known for a generation, Turing's little paper on what would soon be known as artificial intelligence anticipated much of the work of the 1950s and beyond, including both the modeling of the nervous system by Marvin Minsky and others and the automatic theorem proving programs developed by Allen Newell and Herbert Simon.

The "Turing Test"

Turing's most famous contribution to artificial intelligence was a "thought experiment." Working at the University of Manchester as director of programming for its computer project, Turing devised a concept that became known as the Turing test. In its best-known variation, the test involves a human being communicating via a teletype with an unknown party that might be either another person or a computer. If a computer at the other end is sufficiently able to respond in a humanlike way, it may fool the human into thinking it is another person. (In its original form, this was a variant of a test where a person tried to guess the gender of an unknown person.)

This achievement could in turn be considered strong evidence that the computer is truly intelligent.

Turing gives a hypothetical test dialog (Q is a question from the human participant, A is the answer from the unknown participant):

Q: *Please write me a sonnet on the subject of the Forth bridge.*
A: *Count me out on this one. I never could write poetry.*

Q: *Add 34957 to 70764.*
A: *(Pause about 30 seconds and then give as answer) 105621*

Q: *Do you play chess?*
A: *Yes.*

Q: *I have K at my K1, and no other pieces.*
   You have only K at K6 and R at R1. What do you play?
A: *(After a pause of 15 seconds) R-R8 mate.*

In his 1950 article Turing suggested that

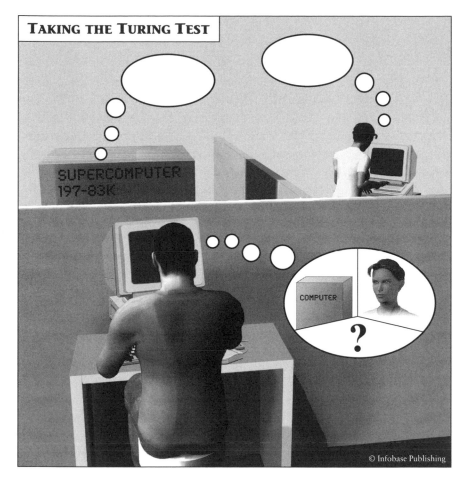

The Turing test invites a person to choose between two hidden communicators—one a human and the other a computer. If the person cannot reliably decide which one is the computer, the machine can be said to have passed the Turing test and demonstrated intelligence.

I believe that in about fifty years' time it will be possible to program computers so well that an average interrogator will have not more than 70 percent chance of making the right identification after five minutes of questioning. I [also] believe that at the end of the [20th] century the use of words and general educated opinion will have altered so much that one will be able to speak of machines thinking without expecting to be contradicted.

Today's computer storage capacity (in both memory and disk) handily exceeds what Turing believed would be available at the end of the century. On the software side, computer programs such as Joseph Weizenberg's ELIZA and later Web "chatterbots" have been able temporarily to fool people they encounter, but no computer program has yet been able to win the annual Loebner Prize by passing the Turing test when subjected to extensive probing questions by a knowledgeable person. It seems that Turing's 1950 prediction would be the first in a series of overoptimistic statements by AI researchers.

Turing and Objections to AI

Considering that computing had barely begun, it is remarkable how much Turing anticipated the debate over the nature of intelligence (both natural and artificial) that continues more than 50 years later. Turing characterized nine possible objections to the possibility of artificial intelligence.

The "theological objection" argues that intelligence resides in some nonmaterial entity (or "soul") that interacts with the body. Without such a soul, no physical structure can show true intelligence. Turing, however, points out that such a distinction between physical and nonmaterial substances seems not to be helpful in understanding phenomena, and that, besides, there is no reason why God (if He exists) might not choose to put a soul in a nonbiological machine.

The "heads in the sand objection" anticipates later critics such as Joseph Weizenbaum in suggesting that even if thinking machines are possible, they should not be built because they would eventually outperform and perhaps even enslave humans. At any rate, humans would lose their unique identity as reasoning beings. Turing questions whether these fears are really justified and more or less defers them to the future.

A more subtle "mathematical objection" to AI suggests that just as mathematicians had shown that there will always be properly formed mathematical assertions that are unprovable, any computer in a Turing test could be asked questions that it could not answer from within the logic of its programming. However, even if humans (perhaps because of their more flexible biological minds) are not subject to his limitation, Turing points out that just because a computer may not be able to answer every question does not mean it cannot think.

Turing also tackles a more subjective problem in the "Argument from Consciousness." He quotes the 1949 Lister Oration by Geoffrey Jefferson, a distinguished professor of neurosurgery, as arguing that

> *Not until a machine can write a sonnet or compose a concerto because of thoughts and emotions felt, and not by the chance fall of symbols, could we agree that machine equals brain—that is, not only write it but know that it had written it. No mechanism could feel (and not merely artificially signal, an easy contrivance) pleasure at its successes, grief when its valves fuse, be warmed by flattery, be made miserable by its mistakes, be charmed by sex, be angry or depressed when it cannot get what it wants.*

Turing replies that, after all, no individual can prove that another person is having a subjective experience of emotion or of consciousness (to "know that it had written"). If a machine can communicate what it says it is experiencing as effectively as a human, there is no reason to accept that the human is conscious but the machine is not.

An alternative to saying that machines cannot think at all is to argue that they lack certain characteristics of human beings, such as the ability to take the initiative, to be creative, to tell right from wrong, to learn, or even to fall in love. Turing questions whether all intelligences are required to have all these characteristics. Since Turing's time, computer programs do seem to have shown some of these characteristics (creativity, learning, and so on) to the extent that they impress human observers. Although some programs and robots have been given "simulated emotions" or drives, they are not

---

ISSUES: IS THE TURING TEST A DEAD END?

The Turing test may appear to be an elegant end run around the question of what constitutes "true" intelligence. Instead of getting caught in a philosophical morass, the experimenter begins with the fact of intelligent human behavior and sees whether a machine can convincingly engage in such behavior.

However, in their essay in Scientific American's book *Understanding AI*, Kenneth Ford and Patrick Hayes compare the quest for artificial intelligence to the quest for "artificial flight" around the turn of the 20th century. Some inventors of the time thought that creating something as birdlike as possible was the way to go, but today's airplanes do not flap their wings as birds do. Human flight was not achieved through imitation of nature but through extending other engineering principles.

Similarly, Ford, Hayes, and other critics of the Turing test point out the Turing test assumes (or at least strongly suggests) that the path to AI is through understanding and learning to imitate human intelligence. This may be dubious because much "intelligent" human behavior may be the arbitrary or accidental result of evolution or social circumstances. Many AI researchers believe that the more productive approach is to identify the logical structures and procedures that can result in successful problem solving or other sophisticated behavior. They do not see the attempt to pass a Turing test as being a worthwhile goal.

---

yet very convincing as being akin to human feelings and experiences.

A final major argument Turing considered is that computers are programmed with discrete states (that is, something that is either on or off, or has a definite quantity) while the human nervous system seems to have "continuous states" in terms of signal levels, chemistry, and so on. Turing points out, however, that a discrete state machine can be programmed to work with as many states as desired, becoming ever more "fine-grained" and approaching a continuous state. There is no reason to suppose that the behavior of the nervous system cannot be simulated accurately. (Besides, those aspects of the nervous system most directly related to cognition may be more like discrete than continuous systems.)

The Final Enigma

Alan Turing was shy and socially awkward, and as a child he had been poor at the usual forms of team sports. However, Turing discovered an aptitude for long-distance running, and in 1945 he joined a local athletic club, soon becoming their best runner, achieving a marathon time only 11 minutes slower than that of the winner in the 1948 Olympics.

However, the master code breaker Turing held a secret that was very dangerous in his time and place: He was gay. In 1952, Turing clumsily stumbled into a set of circumstances that led to his being arrested for homosexual activity, which was illegal and heavily punished at the time. As an alternative to imprisonment, Turing agreed to a course of estrogen injections to suppress the sex drive.

Turing's life began to spiral downward. The side effects of the drug "treatment" were unpleasant, but he seemed to survive them. The revelation of Turing's homosexuality led to considerable social ostracism. Further, with the cold war well under way, the loss of his security clearance deprived Turing of access to some of the most interesting projects in computer design.

Turing struggled to continue his work, which had gone into new fields of mathematics and physics. Turing sought to discover the principles underlying the growth of plants (such as their grouping of leaves following Fibonacci numbers (1, 1, 2, 3, 5, 8 and so on). He also renewed his interest in quantum mechanics.

Although his friends did not seem to detect anything was wrong, apparently the stress proved to be too much. On June 8, 1954, the house cleaner found Turing's body with a half-eaten apple beside his bed. Turing's mother believed that he had carelessly ingested cyanide while performing a chemical experiment, but most observers agree with the coroner's verdict of suicide. The world had lost one of its first and greatest computer scientists in the prime of his career.

Although he would not live to see it, Turing's ideas and assertions would shape much of the agenda of artificial intelligence research in the 1950s and beyond. Alan Turing's many contributions to computer science were honored by his being elected a Fellow of the British Royal Society in 1951 and by the creation of the prestigious Turing Award by the Association for Computing Machinery, given every year since 1966 for outstanding contributions to computer science.

In recent years Turing's fascinating and tragic life has been the subject of several autobiographies and a stage play (later adapted for television as *Breaking the Code*).

Chronology

1912	Alan Turing is born on June 23 in London
1926–1931	Turing spends difficult years at Sherborne, a prep school
1930	Turing is shocked by the death of his friend Christopher Morcom
1931–1934	Turing studies at King's College, Cambridge University. He becomes a Fellow in 1935
1936	Turing publishes "On Computable Numbers"
1938	Turing receives his doctorate at the Institute for Advanced Study at Princeton, having met a number of distinguished mathematicians
1939–1945	Turing works to crack the German Enigma code during World War II
1946	Turing begins work on digital computer design at the National Physical Laboratory.
1948	Turing becomes Deputy Director of the computing laboratory at Manchester University.
1950	Turing publishes a groundbreaking paper on artificial intelligence and devises the Turing test
	Turing begins to explore innovative ideas about growth and form in biology

| 1952 | Turing is arrested as a homosexual and accepts estrogen injections as an alternative to prison |
| 1954 | Turing dies on June 7, an apparent suicide |

Further Reading

Books

Herken, R. *The Universal Turing Machine*. 2nd ed. London: Oxford University Press, 1988.

A description of Turing's conceptual universal computer.

Hodges, A. *Alan Turing: The Enigma*. New York: Simon & Schuster, 1983. Reprinted New York: Walker, 2000.

A good modern biography of Turing that explores some of the more intimate questions of his life.

————. *Turing*. New York: Routledge, 1999.

Primarily discusses Turing's work in terms of its impact on and relation to philosophy.

Lewin, Ronald. *Ultra Goes to War: The First Account of World War II's Greatest Secret Based on Official Documents*. New York: McGraw Hill, 1978.

Gives previously classified details on how the Allied "Ultra" team broke German wartime ciphers, and on how their achievement helped the Allied war effort.

Articles

Turing, Alan M. "Computing Machinery and Intelligence." *Mind*, vol. 49, 1950, pp. 433–460. Also available online. URL: http://www. abelard.org/turpap/turpap.htm. Accessed on August 15, 2006.

Considered the first major published paper on artificial intelligence.

————. "On Computable Numbers, with an Application to the Entscheidungsproblem." *Proceedings of the London Mathematical Society*, vol. 2, no. 42, 1936–1937, pp. 230–265. Also available online. URL: http://www.abelard.org/turpap2/tp2-ie.asp. Accessed on August 15, 2006.

Turing's mathematical proof of the limits of computability; introduces the "universal computer" or Turing Machine.

————. "Intelligent Machinery," in B. Meltzer and D. Michie, eds., *Machine Intelligence 5*. New York: American Elsevier Publishing, 1970, pp. 3–23.

Turing's first (originally unpublished) paper on AI.

"The Turing Test." Stanford Encyclopedia of Philosophy. Available online. URL: http://plato.stanford.edu/entries/turing-test.+ Accessed on August 15, 2006.

Discusses the Turing test and the various philosophical objections to the idea of machine intelligence.

Web Sites

Hodges, Alan. "The Alan Turing Home Page." Available online. URL: http://www.turing.org.uk/turing/Turing.html. Accessed on August 15, 2006.

A large Web site with material on the life and work of Alan Turing, designed to complement the author's book *Alan Turing: The Enigma*.

2
MIND IN A BOX

ALLEN NEWELL AND HERBERT SIMON EXPLORE
REASONING AND DECISION MAKING

As quoted on a Web page at the Carnegie Mellon computer science department, computer scientist and AI pioneer Allen Newell described his work this way:

> *The scientific problem chooses you; you don't choose it. My style is to deal with a single problem, namely, the nature of the human mind. That is the one problem that I have cared about throughout my scientific career, and it will last me all the way to the end.*

This is a reminder that while AI researchers work with programs, computers, and robots to make them behave in intelligent ways, their ultimate goal is often the understanding of human intelligence. Together with mathematician Clifford Shaw, Allen Newell and Herbert Simon would make a key contribution to the early development of AI by demonstrating that a machine could use logic, draw inferences, and make decisions. In turn their work would shed new light on the behavior of human decision makers and organizations. It would also show the power of computer simulation as a tool for understanding and developing practical intelligent systems.

A Vigorous Mind

Allen Newell was born on March 19, 1927, in San Francisco, California. His father was a distinguished professor of radiology at Stanford Medical School. In an interview with Pamela McCorduck, included in her book *Machines Who Think,* Newell describes his father as

> *in many respects a complete man. . . . He'd built a log cabin up in the mountains. . . . He could fish, pan for gold, the whole bit. At the same time, he was the complete intellectual. . . . Within the environment where I was raised, he was a great man. He was extremely idealistic. He used to write poetry.*

Allen Newell and Herbert Simon had a very productive intellectual partnership and explored many aspects of decision making and information processing in machines and humans. (Carnegie-Mellon University)

This example of a wide-ranging intellect seemed to inspire young Newell's own development. Spending summers at his father's log cabin in the Sierra Nevada instilled in Newell a love of the mountains, and for a time he wanted to be a forest ranger when he grew up. The tall, rugged boy excelled at sports, especially football. At the same time Newell flourished in the demanding academic program at San Francisco's elite Lowell High School. When World War II began Newell enlisted in the U.S. Navy. Following the war, he served on one of the ships monitoring the nuclear tests at Bikini Atoll, where he was assigned the task of mapping the distribution of radiation in the area. Working with this esoteric corner of science kindled an interest in science in general and physics in particular. When Newell left the navy he enrolled in Stanford University to study physics. (Newell wrote his first scientific paper, on X-ray optics, in 1949).

While at Stanford Newell took a course from George Polya, a mathematician who had done important work in heuristics, or practical methods for solving problems. The idea that problem solving could be investigated scientifically and developed into a set of principles would be a key to Newell's approach to artificial intelligence later.

Looking for Interesting Problems

Newell's interest in mathematics was more practical than theoretical. As he told Pamela McCorduck, "I was a problem solver, and I wanted a problem you could go out and solve." Fortunately, Newell soon found an opportunity to do just that. While still a graduate student in 1949, Newell also worked at RAND Corporation, a center of innovative research, and he joined the staff in 1950.

With the cold war under way, RAND received generous open-ended funding from the U.S. Air Force and other government agencies. In turn, each department at RAND received funding that it could allocate to its researchers according to whatever projects seemed to be most promising or intriguing.

At RAND, Newell encountered game theory, the study of the resolution of competing interests. (This field had been established by John von Neumann and Oskar Morgenstern earlier that decade and would become rather famous later through the life and work of John Nash.)

Newell also became interested in logistics, the process by which people and materials are moved from place to place. This field was naturally of paramount interest to the military. (It is often said that military amateurs study strategy or tactics, but professionals study logistics.) Newell wrote a paper for the Munitions Board at the Department of Defense titled "The Science of Supply." In it, Newell comes to the conclusion that abstract mathematical network theory could only go so far in understanding logistics. Too much depends on the study of how humans behave in organizations.

Simulating Organizations

In an age increasingly dominated by giant corporations and government agencies, there was an increasing demand for techniques that could enable organizations to function more efficiently. Newell began to work with experiments with individuals in groups who were given simulated problems to solve.

This effort eventually turned into an air force project at the Systems Research Laboratory at RAND that created a simulation of an entire air force early warning station—this at a time when such stations were the key to defense against an anticipated Soviet nuclear bomber attack. Running such a large-scale simulation required creating simulated radar displays, and that in turn meant Newell and his colleagues would have to harness the power of computers. Aided by programmer Clifford Shaw, Newell used a primitive punch-card calculator to print out continuously updated positions for the blips on the simulated radar screen. This project suggested to Newell that more advanced computers might be used to support the study of complex systems such as organizations.

Meeting of the Minds

In 1952, Newell, then 25 years old, met Herbert Simon. They began to work together on a variety of projects where they soon found that their experience and skills fit well together. Simon, 11 years older than Newell, had a broad background in the study of economics and human decision making. Although his life experience was rather different from Newell's, Simon came to share many of the same intellectual interests.

Simon was born on June 15, 1916, in Milwaukee, Wisconsin. His father was an electrical engineer, patent attorney, and inventor; his mother was an accomplished pianist. The young Simon was a bright student who skipped three semesters in high school. In his autobiography *Models of My Life* he would later describe himself as "introspective, bookish, and sometimes lonely" in school—yet paradoxically, he was effective socially, becoming president of most of the clubs he joined. Along the way, Simon mastered several foreign languages and was also an accomplished composer and pianist.

Simon entered the University of Chicago when he was only 17. Simon at first pursued his interest in biology, but his color-blindness and awkwardness in the laboratory discouraged him. He also became fascinated by an introductory economics class but avoided becoming an economics major when he learned he would have to study accounting first. Because he was so far advanced intellectually for his age, Simon was able to meet many requirements by passing examinations rather than attending classes. His habit of "self-study" became firmly fixed.

Simon Sets His Course

While studying for his B.A. in political science (awarded in 1936) Simon studied the operation of the Milwaukee Recreation Department. This study in public administration inspired what would be the core concern of Simon's research career—the process of decision making, whether by people or computers.

After graduation Simon worked for several years for the International City Manager's Association. As an assistant to Clarence Ridley (who had been one of his teachers), Simon helped devise mathematical methods for evaluating the effectiveness or efficiency of municipal services. While doing this work Simon also was introduced to automated information processing in the form of IBM punch-card tabulation equipment. This made him aware of the potential value of the new computing technology that would emerge in the 1940s.

In 1939, Simon moved to the University of California, Berkeley, to head a Rockefeller Foundation–funded study of local government. During this time he also completed the work for his University of Chicago Ph.D. (awarded in 1943). His doctoral dissertation would in 1947 become the book *Administrative Behavior,* an analysis of decision making in the hierarchies of organizations. Later Simon would explain that during this time behaviorism (stimulus-response and conditioning) was king and the analysis of cognitive behavior was out of fashion: "you couldn't use a word like 'mind' in a psychology journal—you'd get your mouth washed out with soap." It

"Johnniac," named for mathematician John von Neumann, was a powerful computer for its time. Nevertheless, researchers such as Allen Newell, Herbert Simon, and Clifford Shaw had very limited computing power at their disposal. (Photo Researchers)

was in this atmosphere that Simon worked toward a psychology that focused on information processing rather than external behavior.

Meanwhile Simon had joined the political science faculty at the Illinois Institute of Technology; in 1946 he became chair of the department. In 1949, he then joined the new business school at Carnegie Institute of Technology in Pittsburgh, which later became Carnegie Mellon University (CMU).

Around that same time, Simon read a book called *Giant Brains* that described the exciting new world of digital computing that had been ushered in after the war by ENIAC and its successors. The author, Edmund Berkeley, also sold a little kit that allowed the user to wire simple computer logic circuits. Simon bought the kit and got a bit of hands-on experience in how computers worked.

Simon and Newell's Opening Moves

Once Simon and Newell had met, the stage was now set for a remarkable scientific collaboration. Newell brought to the table a deep understanding and appreciation of the power of the computer to model and simulate the kinds of processes Simon had been studying in organizations. Simon, who had already come to see the human mind as a sort of information-processing device, now had a partner who could design and code actual programs. The only place where the two researchers did not fit well together was in their working style and hours—Newell loved to pull "all nighters," while Simon preferred a more conventional schedule.

In 1954, Newell attended a RAND seminar in which visiting researcher Oliver Selfridge described a computer system that could recognize and manipulate patterns, such as characters in text. According to Simon, Newell experienced a "conversion experience" in which he realized "that intelligent adaptive systems could be built that were far more complex than anything yet done." He could do this by combining what he had learned about heuristics (problem solving) with bits of simulation and game theory.

Newell decided to use chess as the test bed for his ideas. Researchers such as Alan Turing and Claude Shannon had already made some headway in writing chess programs, but these efforts focused on a relatively mechanical brute force approach to generating and analyzing possible positions following each move.

Newell, however, tried to simulate some of the characteristics that a human player brings to the game, including the ability to search not for the theoretically best move but for a "good enough" move, and the ability to formulate and evaluate short- and long-term goals. For example, a computer chess player might have short-term goals such as clearing a file for its rook, as well as longer-term goals such as taking control of the king side in preparation for an all-out attack on the opponent's king. In 1955 Newell presented his ideas in a conference paper titled "The Chess Machine: An Example of Dealing with a Complex Task by Adaptation." The ultimate result was a chess program called NSS (Newell, Simon, Shaw) that demonstrated the ability to derive moves from general principles and to learn from experience. It was this ability, not the program's extremely modest

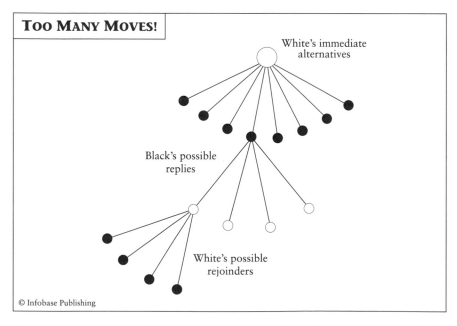

TOO MANY MOVES!

White's immediate alternatives

Black's possible replies

White's possible rejoinders

© Infobase Publishing

Since in chess each possible move has many possible replies, attempting to look ahead soon results in a "combinatorial explosion" where there are too many possibilities for even the fastest computer to consider.

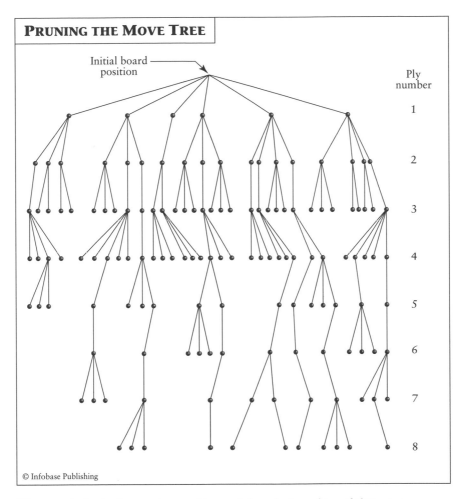

PRUNING THE MOVE TREE

Initial board position

Ply number

1

2

3

4

5

6

7

8

© Infobase Publishing

The practical solution to the combinatorial explosion of possibilities is to develop "pruning" strategies that select only certain sequences of moves for further exploration.

playing skill, that represented an important contribution to AI. (Around this time Newell also predicted that within a decade the chess champion of the world would be a computer. If one accepts the 1997 victory of IBM's Deep Blue over Garry Kasparov as legitimate, Newell's prediction would be off by about three decades.)

I WAS THERE: UNEXPECTED RESULTS

Newell began his own research on organizational behavior by setting up a simple experiment in which a table was divided into partitions so that participants who were assigned a task could not see and talk to each other—they could only communicate by sending simple messages using switches and lights. After running a few sessions, however, Newell discovered that the participants were not acting like the typical bureaucratic types that Simon had been studying. Instead of spending time thrashing out who was in charge and what to do, participants were quietly analyzing the problem, coming up with a solution, and then implementing it. It turned out that Newell had recruited experimental subjects from the most convenient (and least expensive) source—fellow RAND researchers who often volunteered for one another's experiments. Most of the people were mathematicians, and they thus tackled the assigned problem using a logical, rational approach!

As Newell later recalled to Pamela McCorduck:

> . . . I kept trying to enrich the situation so that what would happen would be organizational behavior rather than this highly intellectual behavior. The tasks became more and more complicated so that these guys couldn't simply figure out the problem. But it was hopeless. They were too smart.

Newell gradually realized that for realistic organizational behavior to emerge, the number of participants would have to be greatly increased. With enough people involved and a sufficiently complicated and prolonged task, no individual would be able to visualize the entire problem and its possible solutions. Instead, they would be forced to create organizational structures in order to come to a collective solution.

A Logic Machine

Having developed a program that could cope to some extent at least with the complexities of chess, Newell, Simon, and collaborator Clifford Shaw decided to broaden their approach to automated reasoning into the realm of mathematical proofs. Two promising areas were geometric proofs (including the simple kind taught in high school) and the more arcane, symbolic logic that was exhaustively treated in Bertrand Russell and Alfred North Whitehead's *Principia Mathematica*.

The biggest obstacle the researchers faced in turning their ideas into reality was the primitive state of computer languages and programming techniques at the time. Computers were programmed in a highly detailed (and tedious) machine language where each movement of data had to be precisely specified. Because it was hard to visualize the overall structure of such programs it was very difficult to revise them or make them more flexible.

Simon and Newell decided to address that problem by creating what they would call Information Processing Language. This language would organize data at a much higher level, where it could be understood by humans. Data structures would be flexible, and links between data could be readily made and changed. IPL would make complex AI programs much more practicable. (John McCarthy's list-processing language, Lisp, was being developed around the same time, and it, not IPL, would become the main language for AI research.) Although Simon would constantly contribute ideas, Newell would do the main work in designing and implementing IPL.

With the aid of the new programming language, Newell and Simon began writing a program called the Logic Theory Machine (LTM) that could prove mathematical theorems. By 1956, the program was running and demonstrated several proofs. Rather than using deduction from premise to conclusion, the program worked backward from a hypothesized theorem to the axioms from which it could be proven. In a paper Newell described the LTM as "a complex information processing system . . . capable of discovering proofs for theorems in symbolic logic. This system, in contrast to the systematic algorithms . . . ordinarily employed in computation, relies heavily on heuristic methods similar to those that have been observed in human problem solving activity."

Simon wrote to Bertrand Russell describing how his program could automatically provide proofs found in the *Principia*. As quoted in Simon's autobiography *Models of My Life,* the great mathematician and philosopher replied:

I am delighted to know that Principia Mathematica can now be done by machinery. I wish [coauthor Alfred North] Whitehead and I had known of this possibility before we wasted ten years doing it by hand. I am quite willing to believe that anything in deductive logic can be done by machine.

A little later Simon wrote again to Russell, describing how the program had found a much simpler version of one of the book's more complex proofs. It seemed that computers could not just replicate, but also innovate.

Perhaps the most profound effect of Logic Theorist was summarized by Simon in his autobiography:

We invented a computer program capable of thinking non-numerically, and thereby solved the venerable mind-body problem, explaining how a system composed of matter can have the properties of mind.

In a 1958 paper on problem solving Simon would elaborate, addressing his readers:

I don't mean to shock you. But the simplest way I can summarize is to say that there are now machines that think, that learn and that create. Moreover their ability to do these things is going to increase rapidly until—in a visible future—the range of problems they can handle will be coextensive with [as great as] the range to which the human mind has been applied.

However, as will be seen in the later debate over the validity and significance of AI, the question of whether a machine can truly have a mind would remain open.

The General Problem Solver

Newell, Simon, and Shaw's paper "Elements of a Theory of Human Problem-Solving," published in *Psychological Review,* offered an

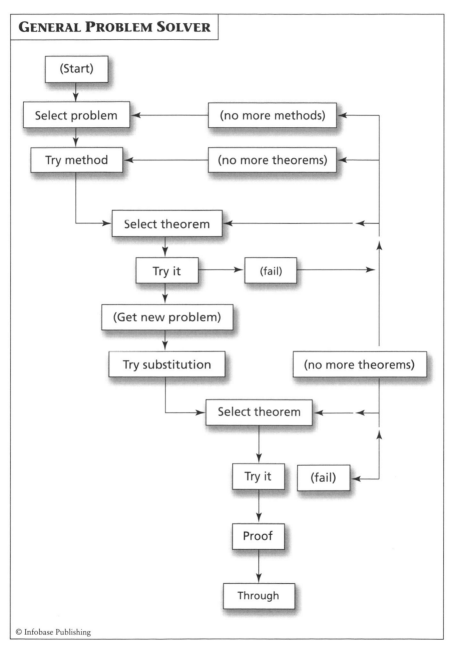

GENERAL PROBLEM SOLVER

(Start)

Select problem ← (no more methods) ←

Try method ← (no more theorems) ←

Select theorem ←

Try it → (fail) →

(Get new problem)

Try substitution

(no more theorems)

Select theorem ←

Try it (fail)

Proof

Through

© Infobase Publishing

This flowchart shows the steps that Newell and Simon's Logic Theorist takes in trying to solve a problem.

PARALLELS: CHESS AND MATHEMATICAL PROOFS

Some critics complain that chess, despite its complexity, has little in common with the real work done by mathematicians or scientists who are seeking to prove a conjecture.

True, there are some differences between the task of a chess player and a theoretician. The chess player is faced with a variety of opening moves, each of which has a number of possible continuations. Although chess openings have been exhaustively studied by chess writers, once the game moves "out of the opening book" there are likely many different strategic and tactical "themes" that the player may try to identify and pursue.

The mathematician, on the other hand, begins with a specific goal (such as to prove that two angles in a geometric figure must be equal). The task becomes to decide what the initial conditions are (for example, that it is a right triangle) and what axioms or already proven theorems (for example, the Pythagorean theorem) to consider. One then creates a chain of reasoning in which each step is justified by what preceded it and in turn allows for a further deduction.

Choosing axioms, theorems, and deductions can be considered to be "moves" in the mathematical chess game. Where a real chess game becomes more like logic is when a "forced" sequence of moves appears. That is, when whatever the opponent does, he or she will be checkmated (or lose a piece, etc.).

A mathematician is unlikely to go through a mental list of any of thousands of possible elements for creating a logic chain. Similarly, even the most powerful computer is limited in how many chess move sequences it can evaluate. A key insight in the work of Newell, Simon, and other AI theorists is that it is possible for a program to determine what logical "moves" are more likely to be relevant to a problem, based on a heuristic or "rule of thumb" or upon previous experience with solving the same type of problem. This strategy for solving logic problems is similar to that adopted in creating an automated chess player that does not rely solely on "brute force" methods.

intriguing tool to psychologists. It suggested that human thinking processes could be viewed as consisting of "programs" similar to those being modeled on computers. Human experimental subjects could "think out loud" to describe their problem-solving process and their procedures could be compared with or simulated by the ones programmed on the machines. The result could be a new systematic exploration of neurological and cognitive processes.

By 1960 Newell and his collaborators had created a more powerful program called the General Problem Solver, or GPS. This program could be given a specification for a "problem domain," a set of operators (ways to manipulate the elements of the problem domain), and guidelines about which operators were generally applicable to various situations. The program could then develop a solution to the problem using appropriate application of the operators. Then, in a further refinement, the program was given the ability to discover new operators and their appropriate use—in other words, it could learn and adapt.

Meanwhile the Newell team had also created a chess-playing program called NSS (named for the last initials of the researchers). While NSS was not as strong a player as the "brute force" programs,

---

I WAS THERE: THE BIRTH OF AI

Computer science professor (and AI pioneer) Edward Feigenbaum recalled to Pamela McCorduck that as a Carnegie student he was taking a course from Herbert Simon called Mathematical Models in the Social Sciences. After the class returned from Christmas vacation in January 1956 Simon came into the classroom and said "Over Christmas Allen Newell and I invented a thinking machine." (He was referring to their development of Logic Theorist, one of the most significant early AI programs.)

Feigenbaum recalls that he and his fellow students were puzzled: "We kind of had an idea of what machines were like. So the words thinking and machines didn't quite fit together, didn't quite make sense."

Simon answered their question by handing out manuals for the IBM 701, an early mainframe computer. He invited them to learn how to program themselves so they could explore what computers could demonstrate about the nature of thinking.

it successfully applied automated problem-solving techniques, making it an "interesting" player.

Expanding the Artificial Mind

During the 1960s and 1970s Newell and Simon delved more deeply into fundamental questions of "knowledge architecture"—how information could be represented within a program in ways such that the program might appear to "understand" it. Newell's "Merlin" program was an ambitious attempt to create a program that could understand AI research itself, being able to demonstrate and explain various other AI programs. Unfortunately, the program never worked very well. However, Newell and Simon's 1972 book *Human Problem-Solving* laid out comprehensive techniques for analyzing how humans verbalized problems and expressed knowledge. This in turn would provide the foundation for the development of expert systems by Edward Feigenbaum and others in the 1980s (see chapter 5, "Harnessing Knowledge"). Newell would become involved in a number of areas besides AI research. One was an attempt to build a simulation of human cognitive psychology called the "Model Human Processor." It was hoped that the simulation would help researchers at the Xerox Palo Alto Research Center (PARC) who were devising what would become the modern computer user interface with mouse-driven windows, menus, and icons. The research would be summarized in a book titled *The Psychology of Human-Computer Interaction*.

Since the early 1970s Newell had a lively interest in the ARPANet (funded by the Defense Department's Advanced Research Projects Agency), which gradually became the Internet. Newell also helped establish the goals for the agency's research in automatic speech recognition. During the 1980s Newell made important contributions to the CMU computer science curriculum and department, and to the establishment of Andrew, the campus computer network.

A General Theory of Thinking

Finally, Newell attempted to draw together the models of cognition (both computer and human) that he and many other researchers had developed. At the heart of the approach was the idea that intelligence could be explained as the manipulation of "physical symbol systems"—sophisticated information processing. (Some later critics would dispute this—see for example chapter 9, "A Philosopher's Challenge.")

Newell's last problem-solving program, SOAR, demonstrated ideas that he explained in his book *Unified Theories of Cognition.* These techniques included learning by grouping or "chunking" elements of the problem, and the ability to break problems into subgoals or subproblems and then working back up to the solutions. Drawing on researchers from a number of different universities, the SOAR project continues today. It remains a tribute to Newell, one of whose maxims expressed in a 1991 talk on "Desires and Diversions" was "choose a project to outlast you."

Getting to "Good Enough"

Meanwhile, Simon brought a rather similar insight to economics. Like mathematicians, economists tended to be abstract in their models. They often wrote about a market where all the participants had perfect or complete knowledge with which they could act in such a way as to maximize profits (or minimize losses). Simon pointed out that in actual business decisions information is incomplete and thus decision makers had to take uncertainty into consideration and arrive at a compromise. He called this behavior or strategy "satisficing" and the overall concept "bounded rationality." Besides limits on available knowledge, Simon stressed that decision making is also strongly influenced by concepts of authority, relationship of subordinates to superiors, loyalty, and by the many different groups with which a particular individual might identify.

Simon's new approach to understanding economic and organizational decision making was presented in his 1976 book *Administrative Behavior.* Simon's work gained in influence through the 1960s and 1970s and would earn him the Nobel Prize in Economics in 1978.

In an interview in 2000 with the *Pittsburgh Post-Gazette* Simon reflected on the relationship between the various aspects of his work:

I like to think that since I was about 19 I have studied human decision making and problem solving. Bounded rationality was the economics part of that. When computers came along, I felt for the first time that I had the proper tools for the kind of theoretical work I wanted to do. So I moved over to that and that got me into psychology.

During the 1980s Simon continued his research and writing, moving seamlessly between economics, psychology, and computer science and helping foster connections between the disciplines in the curriculum at CMU. Simon also played a key role in creating a prestigious computer science department and a robotics institute at Carnegie Mellon. Simon made an equally important contribution to the university's Graduate School of Industrial Administration as well as contributing to the departments of social sciences, philosophy, statistics, and even physics.

In addition to completing the second volume of a book called *Models of Thought* Simon also published an autobiography, *Models of My Life*. In his introduction to the latter book he tried to explain how he had approached his multifaceted work:

I have been a scientist, but in many sciences. I have explored mazes, but they do not connect into a single maze. My aspirations do not extend to achieving a single consistency in my life. It will be enough if I can play each of my roles creditably, borrowing sometimes from one for another, but striving to represent fairly each character when he has his turn on stage.

A Rich Legacy

Newell died on July 19, 1992. He had published 10 books and more than 250 papers and was the recipient of many honors. In 1975, he received the ACM Turing Award for his contributions to artificial intelligence. In turn the ACM with sponsorship of the American Association for Artificial Intelligence established the Newell Award for "contributions that have breadth within computer science, or that bridge computer science and other disciplines." Just before his death Newell was also awarded the National Medal of Science.

In addition to the 1978 Nobel Prize in economics Simon has received many other awards and positions. These include the American Psychological Association Distinguished Scientific Contribution Award (1969), the Association for Computing Machinery Turing Award (1975), shared with Alan Newell, and the National Medal of Science (1986). Simon died on February 9, 2001.

Together, Allen Newell and Herbert Simon created some of the first demonstrations that at least some aspects of reasoning and perhaps intelligence itself could be modeled in computer programs. In turn, they used what they learned to create theories about human cognition and problem solving.

Chronology

1916	Herbert Simon is born in Milwaukee, Wisconsin, on June 15
1927	Allen Newell is born in San Francisco on March 19
1936	Simon graduates from the University of Chicago with a B.A. in political science
1939	Simon goes to the University of California, Berkeley, to study local government
1942	Newell serves in the U.S. Navy and later helps monitor radiation from nuclear tests
1943	Simon receives his doctorate in political science from the University of Chicago
1949	Newell attends Stanford University as a physics major, as well as working at RAND Corporation. In the next few years he will write reports on organizational theory and logistics (supply).
	Simon joins the business school at the Carnegie Institute of Technology in Pittsburgh (later Carnegie Mellon University), where he will spend the rest of his career

1952	Newell and Simon meet and discover their mutual interest in how the human mind processes information
1954	After attending a seminar on artificial intelligence, Newell becomes inspired to pursue the field
1955	Newell publishes his ideas for a chess-playing machine that can learn
	Newell moves to Carnegie Mellon University
1956	Newell, Simon, and Clifford Shaw demonstrate Logic Theorist, a program that could prove mathematical theorems. The program uses their new IPL, or "Information Processing Language."
1960	Newell, Simon, and Shaw create General Problem Solver, a program that can deal with a variety of mathematical challenges
1978	Simon receives the Nobel Prize in Economics
1980s	Newell publishes *Unified Theories of Cognition* and begins to develop SOAR, an advanced architecture for problem solving and cognition
1992	Allen Newell dies on July 19
2001	Herbert Simon dies on February 9

Further Reading

Books

McCorduck, Pamela. *Machines Who Think*. Revised edition. Natick, Mass.: A. K. Peters, 2004.
> Engaging accounts of AI pioneers and their work, with chapter 6 devoted to Newell and Simon.

Newell, Alan. *Unified Theories of Cognition*. Cambridge, Mass.: Harvard University Press, 1994.
> Newell summarizes a lifetime of work in understanding human and artificial intelligence and introduces SOAR, "an architecture for general cognition."

Rosenblum, Paul S. [and others], ed. *The Soar Papers: Research on Integrated Intelligence.* Cambridge, Mass.: MIT Press, 1993.
> Extensive discussions of main aspects of the SOAR project, representing an important contribution to AI research in the 1980s and early 1990s.

Simon, Herbert. *Administrative Behavior.* Fourth edition. New York: Macmillan, 1997.
> Most recent version of Simon's ground-breaking description of human decision making in organizations.

———. *Models of My Life.* New York: Basic Books, 1991.
> Simon's autobiography, including vivid accounts of his key work.

Articles

"Allen Newell, 1927–1992." Carnegie Mellon University Computer Science Department. Available online. URL: http://www.cs.cmu.edu/afs/cs/misc/mosaic/common/omega/Web/csd/newell.html. Accessed on August 15, 2006.
> Gives a quote and some reflections summarizing Newell's approach to life and work.

Holden, Constance. "The Rational Optimist: Will Computers Ever Think Like People? This Expert in Artificial Intelligence Asks, Why Not?" *Psychology Today,* vol. 20, October 1986, pp. 54 ff.
> A look at the possibilities of AI based on Newell and Simon's work.

Newell, Allen, Simon, Herbert, and Clifford Shaw. "Elements of a Theory of Human Problem-Solving." *Psychological Review,* July 1958.
> Suggests ways in which computers could be used to study and stimulate human problem-solving strategies.

Simon, Herbert A. "Allen Newell, March 19, 1927–July 19, 1992" Biographical Memoirs, National Academy of Science. Available online. URL: http://stills.nap.edu/readingroom/books/biomems/anewell.html. Accessed on August 15, 2006.
> Simon thoughtfully describes his work with his long time scientific partner.

———. "Autobiography." Available online. URL: http://www.nobel.se/economics/laureates/1978/simon-autobio.html. Accessed on August 15, 2006.
> Brief autobiography of Simon as of the time he won the Nobel Prize.

Spice, Byron. "CMU's Simon Reflects on How Computers Will Continue to Shape the World." 16 October 2000. Pittsburgh Post-Gazette.com. Available online. URL: http://www.post-gazette.com/regionstate/20001016simon2.asp. Accessed on August 15, 2006.
Simon looks back at his work and suggests ways in which humans may cope with computer advances in the future.

Web Sites

"Herbert A. Simon, 1916–2001." New School, Economics Department. Available online. URL: http://cepa.newschool.edu/het/profiles/simon.htm. Accessed on August 15, 2006.
Provides numerous links relating to Simon's life, work, and related interests.
"Herbert Simon Collection." Carnegie Mellon University. Available online. URL: http://diva.library.cmu.edu/Simon. Accessed on August 15, 2006.
Provides online access to an extensive collection of publications and correspondence by or relating to Herbert Simon.

3
I HAVE A LITTLE LIST

JOHN MCCARTHY CREATES TOOLS FOR AI

At the dawn of the computer age Alan Turing, John von Neumann, and Claude Shannon had made intriguing suggestions about how the new machines might someday do much more than just compute. But while crunching numbers was relatively straightforward and depended mainly on a steady improvement of hardware, manipulating symbols to solve advanced math and logic problems would require the development of new computer languages and tools. John McCarthy's list-processing language, Lisp, would give AI researchers a much more powerful way to represent data and logical operations in the computer memory.

John McCarthy developed many tools for AI research, including the computer language Lisp. (Mel Lindstrom Photography)

Radical Roots

John McCarthy was born on September 4, 1927, in Boston, Massachusetts. His father, an Irish immigrant, was active in radical labor politics. His mother, a Lithuanian Jew, was equally militant, involved in women's suffrage and other issues. Both were members of the Communist Party, making young McCarthy what would become known as a "red diaper baby." However, McCarthy's father was also an inventor and technological enthusiast, and the boy grew up reading books that promised a future where socialism united with technology would transform the world.

The family moved to California when the boy was still young, in part because his prodigal intellect was accompanied by poor health. He skipped over much of grade school, attended Belmont High School in Los Angeles, and graduated when he was only 15.

While in high school McCarthy became increasingly interested in mathematics. As a junior, he read a course catalog for the California Institute of Technology and bought all the calculus books assigned to freshman and sophomore mathematics classes. McCarthy read the books and worked through the exercises. In 1944, when McCarthy enrolled in Caltech, he petitioned successfully to skip the first two years of college math!

McCarthy entered the California Institute of Technology in 1944 to major in mathematics, but he was called into the army for awhile, where he served as a clerk, returning to Caltech to get his bachelor's degree in 1948.

A Possible Machine

As a graduate student, McCarthy had an encounter that would shape his career. At a Cal Tech symposium McCarthy heard a lecture by the great mathematician and computer scientist John von Neumann on "self-replicating automata." The notion that a machine could be designed to make a copy of itself fascinated McCarthy. He asked himself whether such a machine could become intelligent.

In 1949, McCarthy entered the doctoral program in mathematics at Princeton. By then he had had further thoughts on intelligent machines. McCarthy recalled to Dennis Shasha and Cathy Lazere that

> *I considered an intelligent thing as a finite automaton that was connected to an environment that was itself a finite automaton. I made*

an appointment to see John von Neumann. He was encouraging. He said, "Write it up, write it up." But I didn't write it up because I didn't feel it was really good.

By "finite automaton" McCarthy meant a mechanism that had a fixed number of "states" together with rules for switching from one state to a succeeding state. For example, a traffic light is a simple finite automaton with basic rules: If its state is "yellow," for example, its corresponding rule guarantees that the next state will be "red." A more sophisticated automaton, however, changes state not only according to internal rules but also according to the state it encounters in the environment. For example, a driver might be thought of as such an automaton, paying attention not only to traffic lights but also to the actions of other drivers. (In 1955, McCarthy and Claude Shannon would coauthor the book *Automata Studies*. McCarthy's contribution would focus on the possibility of automatic learning programs.)

McCarthy soon decided that the automaton model could not really be used to describe human or machine intelligence, but it had gotten him thinking about the characteristics of intelligent machines at a time when only a handful of other pioneers (such as Alan Turing, Claude Shannon, and von Neumann) were beginning to sketch out proposals and projects in machine intelligence.

McCarthy then earned his Ph.D. at Princeton University in 1951. During the early 1950s he held teaching posts at Stanford University, Dartmouth College, and the Massachusetts Institute of Technology.

Dartmouth and the "Birth" of AI

Although he seemed destined for a prominent career in pure mathematics, McCarthy had another fateful encounter when he gained some experience with computers while working during the summer of 1955 at an IBM laboratory. McCarthy was intrigued with the potential of the machines for higher-level reasoning and intelligent behavior. More than just being intrigued, he was determined that the still-scattered researchers and their efforts be brought together at an extended conference at Dartmouth University during the summer of 1956. After thinking about what to call this emerging new field of science and technology, he hit upon the phrase "artificial intelligence." It succinctly challenged everyone to consider two things that were not often thought of as belonging together: machines, with their presumably fixed, mechanical action, and "intelligence"—thought by many to be a subtle, flexible quality found only in humans and perhaps certain "higher" animals.

Together with Shannon, Marvin Minsky (himself to become a key figure in AI), and computer designer Nat Rochester from IBM, McCarthy obtained funding and organized the conference. Considering the revolutionary impact of the research that would be inspired by the meeting, the $7,500 budget obtained from the Rockefeller Foundation seems quite modest.

The goals of the research were not so modest, however. The conference proposal said that they would "proceed on the basis of the conjecture that every aspect of learning or any other feature of intelligence can in principle be so precisely described that a machine can be made to simulate it." For his portion of the conference, McCarthy said in his later interview with Pamela McCorduck that he wanted

> to attempt to construct an artificial language which a computer can be programmed to use on problems requiring conjecture and self-reference. It should correspond to English in the sense that short English statements about the given subject matter should have short correspondents in the language and so should short arguments or conjectural arguments. I hope to try to formulate a language having these properties and in addition to contain the notions of physical object, event, etc., with the hope that using this language it will be possible to program a machine to learn to play games well and to do other tasks.

This was certainly an ambitious project in itself. Forty years later McCarthy would tell Shasha and Lazere that "the goals that I had for that conference were entirely unrealistic. I thought that major projects could be undertaken during the course of a summer conference."

At the time of the Dartmouth Conference McCarthy was working on a chess-playing program. Because of its complexity, chess was an attractive subject for many early AI researchers. McCarthy invented a method for searching through the possible moves at a given point of the game and "pruning out" those that would lead to clearly bad positions. This "alpha-beta heuristic" would become a standard part of the repertoire of computer game analysis.

One advantage of having such a long career (McCarthy is nearly 80 years old as of 2006) is the opportunity to see how long-range projects work out. In 1997, the special IBM Deep Blue processor defeated world chess champion Garry Kasparov in a match. However, for McCarthy (and many other AI researchers), the development of an intelligent approach to play is much more important than sheer playing strength. In his article "What Is Artificial Intelligence?" on his Stanford Web page, McCarthy laments that

Unfortunately, the competitive and commercial aspects of making computers play chess have taken precedence over using chess as a scientific domain. It is as if the geneticists after 1910 had organized fruit fly races and concentrated their efforts on breeding fruit flies that could win these races.

Lisp

Beyond chess and what it taught about evaluating the branching tree of possible moves, McCarthy was also considering a practical problem. The programming tools of the time simply weren't up to the task of representing complex logical conditions and operations. In 1956, John Backus and his team at IBM had introduced FORTRAN (FORmula TRANSlator), a language that could be used to program numerical expressions. The language would prove to be a workhorse for at least two generations of scientific and engineering programmers.

Meanwhile McCarthy had been helping Herbert Gelernter and Nathaniel Rochester to develop a program that could prove geometry theorems. Such a program needed a way to represent lists of logical conditions and rules for manipulating them. McCarthy suggested that Gelernter and his assistant Carl Gerberich build an extension to FORTRAN that could manipulate such lists. (Meanwhile, as described in chapter 2, "Mind in a Box," Alan Newell, Herbert Simon, and J. C. Shaw were working on their own list-based language, IPL or Information Processing Language.)

McCarthy found that FORTRAN-based list processing was too cumbersome. For one thing, it lacked recursion, or the ability of an expression to refer to itself. With recursion, some problems can be made to unravel like a trick knot.

What is most important for AI research is that Lisp is general and flexible enough to allow almost any desired structure to be represented and built. (It is true that Lisp expressions with their multiple

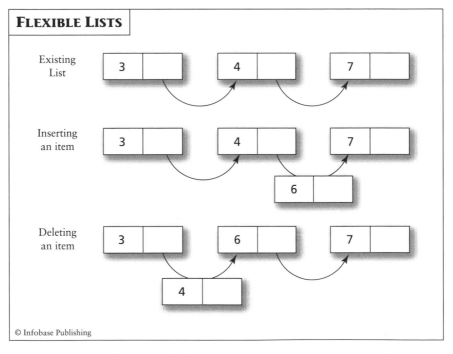

FLEXIBLE LISTS

Existing List

Inserting an item

Deleting an item

© Infobase Publishing

In a linked list, each item in the list has a "pointer" to the next item. This structure makes it easy to insert or remove items without having to move them in the computer's memory.

layers of enclosing parentheses can be intimidating to beginning programmers.)

According to one mathematician quoted in the book *Scientific Temperaments* by Philip J. Hilts:

> *The new expansion of man's view of the nature of mathematical objects, made possible by LISP, is exciting. There appears to be no limit to the diversity of problems to which LISP will be applied. It seems to be a truly general language, with commensurate computing power.*

Framing the Question

McCarthy had created Lisp as a powerful tool for the young AI community. However, he believed that the purpose of tools was not to exist, but to be used to do new and interesting things. In 1959, McCarthy published a paper titled "Programs with Common Sense." In it, he looked forward to programs that had enough of a database of knowledge of relationship of ideas that they could make valid deductions. He gives as an example a person who needs to get from his office to the airport knowing that the way to do so is to go to his car and then drive it to the airport. This presupposes that the program has concepts such as "travel" and "vehicle" and understands how to get from the "here" state to the "there" state.

In discussion of the paper, a noted linguist named Yehoshua Bar-Hillel criticized McCarthy's idea of giving computer programs the ability to make commonsense deductions. McCarthy agreed that he had not gone deeply enough into the implications of designing such a program. The way facts are framed is crucial—for example, does the program know about alternatives such as taking a taxi instead of the car? As Shasha and Lazere note, McCarthy realized that ". . . Whenever we program a computer to learn from experience, we build into the program a sort of epistemology." (Epistemology is the branch of philosophy that deals with how one comes to know things.) Indeed, as will be seen later in this book, a variety of AI pioneers would take up the challenge of encoding understanding in

Connections: SHRDLU and the "Blocks World"

SHRDLU version UMR-1.0
Loaded 4/23/2006 in CLISP 1999-07-22 (July 1999)

READY
SHOW

This is a modern Windows version of SHRDLU, the program that "understands" objects and their relative positions and can explain its actions.

During the 1960s, considerable progress was made by researchers who were trying to get computers to understand a more natural sort of language than the cryptic commands normally used in programming. One of the most interesting programs was Terry Winograd's SHRDLU, a program that manipulates imaginary blocks using an understanding of both basic English syntax and the properties of objects. The program can ask the user questions if it is not sure which object is being referenced. It also "understands" concepts such as what objects can support (hold up) other objects.

The following is a brief bit of dialogue between a person and a computer running SHRDLU:

Person: PICK UP A BIG RED BLOCK.

a form that can enable a computer program to reason in a way that takes common sense into consideration.

As McCarthy's work continued in the 1960s, he brought two new concepts to bear on the problem. One is "situation calculus." This is rather similar to the finite state machine discussed earlier, in that it specifies a current situation (in which a number of things are true) and tries to apply rules to bring about a desired new situation (goal).

Computer: OK. (does it)

Person: GRASP THE PYRAMID.

Computer: I DON'T UNDERSTAND WHICH PYRAMID YOU MEAN.

Person: FIND A BLOCK WHICH IS TALLER THAN THE ONE YOU ARE HOLDING AND PUT IT INTO THE BOX.

Computer: BY "IT," I ASSUME YOU MEAN THE BLOCK WHICH IS TALLER THAN THE ONE I AM HOLDING.

Computer: OK. (does it)

Person: WHAT DOES THE BOX CONTAIN?

Computer: THE BLUE PYRAMID AND THE BLUE BLOCK.

Person: WHAT IS THE PYRAMID SUPPORTED BY?

Computer: THE BOX.

Person: HOW MANY BLOCKS ARE NOT IN THE BOX?

Computer: FOUR OF THEM.

Person: IS AT LEAST ONE OF THEM NARROWER THAN THE ONE WHICH I TOLD YOU TO PICK UP?

Computer: YES, THE RED CUBE.

Person: IS IT SUPPORTED?

Computer: YES, BY THE TABLE.

Person: CAN THE TABLE PICK UP BLOCKS?

Computer: NO.

For example, a person might want to fly from New York to London. An automated flight-booking program would take the original situation (the person is in New York, is willing to spend a certain amount of money, and needs to get to London on a certain day.) The program would then combine the situation with facts it knows about how airlines work and develop a plan to get to the goal (the person has a ticket that gets her to London on time.)

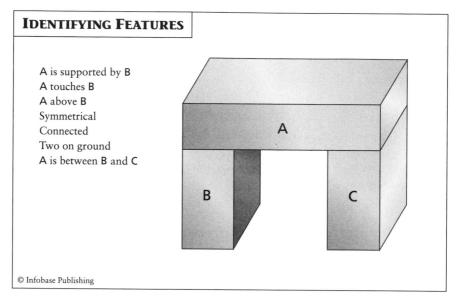

IDENTIFYING FEATURES

A is supported by B
A touches B
A above B
Symmetrical
Connected
Two on ground
A is between B and C

A

B   C

© Infobase Publishing

SHRDLU's knowledge base includes concepts of position, connectedness, and support that enable it to "understand" and manipulate the block structures.

McCarthy and researcher Patrick Hayes of the University of Edinburgh introduced a second idea that helps explain how facts about the situation can be organized: the frame. A frame is a set of things "that don't change when a particular situation occurs." To return to the airline example, regardless of the particular circumstances such as origin, destination, and arrival time, a program would access frames that indicate facts such as "you need a ticket to board a plane." McCarthy believed that a robust program could use frames to determine what was likely true while retaining the ability to incorporate facts that turn out to be exceptions to the rule. (McCarthy called this principle "circumscription," and it reflects the way people have to make many assumptions in order to get through daily life.)

McCarthy also contributed to the development of ALGOL, a language that would in turn greatly influence modern procedural languages such as C. He helped develop new ways for people to use computers. Consulting with Bolt Beranek and Newman (the company that would later build the beginnings of the Internet), McCarthy helped design time-sharing, a system that allowed many users to share the same computer, bringing down the cost of computing and making it accessible to more people. He also sought to make computers more interactive, designing a system called THOR that used video display terminals. Indeed, he pointed the way to the personal computer in a 1972 paper on "The Home Information Terminal."

In his 2003 article "Problems and Projections in CS [Computer Science] for the Next 49 Years" McCarthy noted that Lisp and its programming tools still have advantages over modern languages such as C++ and Java. Lisp expressions are easier to parse (identify component parts), and Lisp programs can change their own structure depending on the conditions they "see" when they run. McCarthy has also made an interesting suggestion that programs communicate with users and each other through "speech acts"—making requests, asking questions, even making commitments or promises. This use of a more natural language would have the potential to improve communication greatly between people and machines and would also help in designing "helper" programs or agents (see chapter 7, "At Your Service").

Reflections and Rewards

By the 1970s AI research was being carried on by major groups at MIT (headed by Marvin Minsky), Carnegie Mellon (Newell and Simon), and McCarthy at Stanford. However, McCarthy had misgivings about what he considered to be a troubling lack of communication and cooperation in the AI field. He remarked to Pamela McCorduck that

> I don't think we talk to each other as much as we should. We tend to have these separate empires which exchange ideas by means of ambassadors, in the form of graduate students. . . . If we were really going to understand what everyone else is doing, we'd have to spend a lot of time together—none of us has an excessive talent in understanding other peoples' points of view. There's a tendency after starting a discussion to say, ah yes, this suggests something I want to work on, and the real desire is to get off alone and work on it.

McCarthy's life has taken him beyond intellectual adventures. He has climbed mountains, flown planes, and jumped from them, too. Although he came to reject his parents' Marxism and the doctrinaire stance of the radical left, since the 1960s McCarthy has also been active in political issues. In recent years he has been especially concerned that computer technology be used to promote rather than suppress democracy and individual freedom. He has suggested that the ability to review and, if necessary, correct all computer files containing personal information be established as a fundamental constitutional right.

In 1971, McCarthy received the prestigious A. M. Turing Award from the Association for Computing Machinery. In the 1970s and 1980s he taught at Stanford and mentored a new generation of AI researchers. He has remained a prominent spokesperson for AI, arguing against critics such as philosopher Hubert Dreyfus who claimed that machines could never achieve true intelligence. As of 2001, McCarthy has been Professor Emeritus of Computer Science at Stanford University.

McCarthy on the Future of AI

At a time when both proponents and critics of AI have tended to make extravagant claims, McCarthy seems to take a methodical, pragmatic approach. In an article titled "What Is Artificial Intelligence?" on his Web page at Stanford, McCarthy summarizes the approach to AI as follows:

Progress in AI is made by

1. *Representing more kinds of general facts about the world by logical formulas or in other suitable ways.*

2. *Identifying intellectual mechanisms, e.g. those beyond logical deduction involved in commonsense reasoning.*

3. *Representing the approximate concepts used by people in commonsense reasoning.*

4.   *Devising better algorithms for searching the space of pos-*
     sibilities, e.g. better ways of making computers do logical
     deduction.

There has been much debate over whether a computer can ever be
"conscious" in the way humans seem to be. McCarthy suggests that
sophisticated computer programs will include introspection, or the
ability to analyze their own behavior and explain how they arrive at
a given conclusion. (Indeed, many AI programs can already do that
in a limited way.) McCarthy suggests that, "This will look like consciousness to an external observer just as human intelligent behavior
leads to our ascribing consciousness to each other."

Looking back at this long career, how does McCarthy assess the
future of AI? On his Web page, McCarthy offers a judicious sum-
mary. He notes that

> *A few people think that human-level intelligence can be achieved*
> *by writing large numbers of programs of the kind people are now*
> *writing and assembling vast knowledge bases of facts in the lan-*
> *guages now used for expressing knowledge. However, most AI*
> *researchers believe that new fundamental ideas are required, and*
> *therefore it cannot be predicted when human-level intelligence will*
> *be achieved.*

This son of radicals has not lost his social consciousness. McCarthy
is aware of the challenges that a breakthrough in AI might bring. In
his 2003 article for the *Journal of the ACM* McCarthy suggests that
"the main danger is of people using AI to take unfair advantage of
other people. However we won't know enough to regulate it until we
see what it actually looks like."

As for the question of when human-level artificial intelligence
will arrive, McCarthy is a bit more pessimistic than Ray Kurzweil
(see chapter 10, "When Everything Changes"). In his 2003 article
McCarthy says, "I'll guess 0.5 probability in the next 49 years, but
a 0.25 probability that 49 years from now, the problems will be just
as confusing as they are today."

Chronology

1927	John McCarthy is born on September 4 in Boston
1944	McCarthy enters the California Institute of Technology (Caltech) as a math major, but then serves several years in the U.S. Army as a clerk
1948	Having returned to Caltech, McCarthy gets a bachelor's degree in mathematics
1951	McCarthy receives his Ph.D. in mathematics from Princeton
1955	McCarthy works at an IBM laboratory and gains computer experience McCarthy coins the term "artificial intelligence"
1956	McCarthy organizes the Dartmouth summer conference on artificial intelligence, bringing together key players and the agenda for the field
1956	McCarthy works on a chess-playing program
1958	McCarthy develops the Lisp (list processor) computer language
1959	McCarthy publishes the paper "Programs with Common Sense."
1960s	McCarthy helps develop time-sharing and interactive computer displays McCarthy and other researchers begin to use the idea of "frames" to develop programs that can deal with real-world situations
1971	McCarthy receives the A. M. Turing Award
1970s	McCarthy teaches at Stanford
2001	McCarthy becomes professor emeritus of computer science at Stanford
2003	McCarthy makes cautious predictions for progress in computer science and AI

Further Reading

Books

McCorduck, Pamela. *Machines Who Think*. Natick, Mass.: A. K. Peters, 2004.
> Revised edition of her engaging account of the work of John McCarthy and other AI pioneers.

Shasha, Dennis, and Cathy Lazere. *Out of Their Minds: The Lives and Discoveries of 15 Great Computer Scientists*. New York: Springer-Verlag, 1995.
> Includes interesting in-depth profiles of computer scientists including AI pioneers John McCarthy, W. Daniel Hillis, Edward Feigenbaum, and Douglas Lenat.

Articles

Colby, Paul. "Famous Figures in AI: John McCarthy." Available online. URL: http://www.cs.jcu.edu.au/ftp/web/teaching/Subjects/cp3210/1998/Assignments/StudentEssays.html#McCarthy-Colby. Accessed on August 15, 2006.
> Summarizes McCarthy's chief contributions to the theory of AI, including ideas about automated reasoning and the development of LISP.

McCarthy, John. "Problems and Projections for CS in the Next 49 Years." *Journal of the ACM*, vol. 50, January 2003, pp. 73–79.
> McCarthy provides a valuable summary of computer science developments and prospects for breakthroughs in AI.

———. "What Is Artificial Intelligence?" Stanford Computer Science Department. Available online. URL: http://www-formal.stanford.edu/jmc/whatisai/whatisai.html. Accessed on August 15, 2006.
> McCarthy answers basic questions about the field and suggests some resources.

Web Sites

"John McCarthy's Home Page." Available online. URL: http://www.formal.stanford.edu/jmc. Accessed on August 15, 2006.
> McCarthy's home page has many references and reflections on interesting recent work, showing a mind that remains lively and active even as he approaches 80 years of age.

SIMULATED BRAINS

MARVIN MINSKY'S JOURNEY FROM NEURAL
NETWORKS TO MULTIPLE MINDS

To many philosophers and theologians the human mind is a unique and mysterious entity. To AI pioneer Marvin Minsky, the mind is the brain, a "meat machine." However one should not say "*only* a machine," because after decades of teasing out the way perception and information is processed in the brain, Minsky has created a theory that talks about there being many different entities that make up the mind.

Starting in the 1950s, Minsky played a key role in the establishment of artificial intelligence (AI) as a discipline. Combining cognitive psychology and computer science, Minsky developed ways to make computers function in more "brainlike" ways and then offered provocative insights about how the human brain itself might be organized. As he told interviewer John Brockman in 1998, "My goal is making machines that think—by understanding how people think."

Minsky was born in New York City on August 9, 1927. His father was an ophthalmologist—in a memoir he later wrote about his invention of the "Confocal Scanning Microscope," Minsky notes that "our home was simply *full* of lenses, prisms, and diaphragms. I took all his instruments apart, and he quietly put them together again." Minsky's father was also a musician and a painter, making for a rich cultural environment.

Minsky proved to be a brilliant science student at the Fieldston School, the Bronx High School of Science, and the Phillips Academy.

Marvin Minsky's long career has brought to light many provocative ideas about the nature of intelligence, including the possibility that human intelligence emerges from a "society of mind."

(He would later recall that, "As long as I can remember, I was entranced by all kinds of machinery.")

Experiencing Science at Harvard

Before he could go to college World War II intervened, and Minsky enlisted in the U.S. Navy, entering electronics training in 1945 and 1946. He then went to Harvard University, where he received a B.A. in 1950. Although he had majored in mathematics at Harvard and then went to Princeton for graduate study in that field, Minsky was also interested in biology, neurology, genetics, and psychology as well as many other fields of science. (His study of the operation of crayfish claws would later transfer to an interest in robot manipulators.)

Minsky recalled in his microscope memoir that during those early Harvard years

perhaps the most amazing experience of all was in a laboratory course wherein a student had to reproduce great physics experiments of the past. To ink a zone plate onto glass and see it focus on a screen; to watch a central fringe emerge as the lengths of two paths become the same; to measure those lengths to the millionth part with nothing but mirrors and beams of light—I had never seen any things so strange.

Minsky's encounter with Harvard's fertile and diverse research community helped reinforce his wide-ranging enthusiasm for the idea of science and of scientific exploration. He learned to move fluidly between the physical and life sciences, seeing common patterns and suggestive relationships.

Minsky had become particularly fascinated by the most complex machine known to humankind—the human brain. Minsky was not satisfied with theories (whether philosophical or psychoanalytic) that viewed the mind as something that had a nonphysical component that made it somehow unique. In reaction Minsky would later describe the brain as a "meat machine."

However, Minsky found the most popular mechanistic psychology (the behaviorism of B. F. Skinner), to be unsatisfactory because it focused only on behavior, ignoring the brain itself entirely. On the other hand low-level neurological or physiological study of the brain could say little about how thought processes actually worked. What was needed was a connection between the "circuitry" and observed processing of information.

Hunting the SNARC

Minsky began to apply mathematical models to develop a "stochastic" or random probability theory to explain how the brain responds to stimuli. (A Canadian researcher, Donald Hebb, turned out to have developed similar ideas independently.)

In 1951, Minsky and Dean Edmonds designed SNARC, the Stochastic Neural-Analog Reinforcement Computer. At the time, it was known that the human brain contains about 100 billion neurons, and that each neuron can form connections to as many as a thousand neighboring ones. Neurons respond to electronic signals that jump across a gap (called a synapse) and into electrode-like dendrons, thus forming connections with one another. But little was known about what caused particular connections to form, or how the formation of some connections made others more probable. It was also unclear how the networks of connections related to the brain's most important task—learning. In general, Minsky was surprised to find out how little researchers knew about how the brain actually did its work.

Since it was known that the brain used electrical signaling, Minsky decided to create an electrical model that might capture some of the brain's most basic behavior. SNARC worked much like a living brain. Its electrical elements responded to signals in much the same way as the brain's neurons do. The machine was given a task (in this case, solving a maze), but, unlike a computer, was not given a program that told it how to perform it. Instead, the artificial neurons were started with random connections. However, if a particular connection brought the machine closer to its goal, the connection was "reinforced" (given a higher value that made it more likely to persist). Gradually a network of such reinforced connections formed, enabling SNARC to accomplish its task. In other words, SNARC had "learned" how to do something, even though it only had a few hundred vacuum tubes in place of the brain's millions of neurons.

Minsky then used the results of his research for his thesis for his Ph.D. in mathematics (received in 1954). When a member of the dissertation committee complained that Minsky's work might not really be mathematics, John von Neumann replied that, ". . . if it isn't now, it will be someday."

Perceptrons and Neural Networks

Von Neumann's endorsement seemed to be prophetic. In 1957, Frank Rosenblatt and his team at Cornell University built the Perceptron, a relatively simple system in which a layer of "neurons" (with real or simulated sensors) attempt to classify input data (such as a visual pattern). The inputs can be adjusted or "weighted" along with a "bias" until the output represents the correct identification (for example, that the graphic pattern is the letter *A*).

Minsky, however, had growing misgivings about the direction of this research. He and coauthor Seymour Papert's 1969 book *Perceptrons* showed mathematically that the Perceptron could not deal with certain logical operations, such as XOR. (XOR, or "exclusive OR" is an operation where the result is true when one, and only one of the two inputs is true.) It turned out, however, that a multiple-layer neural network was not subject to these limitations, and Minsky and Papert were later criticized for discouraging neural network research until its resurgence in the 1980s. Today neural networks are used in a variety of applications (particularly for pattern recognition).

Emergence of AI Research

In addition to his doctoral degree, Harvard also gave Minsky a valuable junior fellowship, which allowed him to pursue the research of his choice. Because work on brain structure and the organization of intelligence did not fit into any existing department, the independence the fellowship provided was particularly important.

In 1956, the Dartmouth Summer Research Project in Artificial Intelligence brought Minsky together with John McCarthy, Claude Shannon, Allen Newell, and other researchers who were developing computer programs that could carry out reasoning processes (such as proving theorems in geometry) and manipulate symbols and language.

These few short weeks seemed to be full of promise for the future of AI. Like astronomy in the wake of Galileo's telescope, new techniques and applications appeared wherever the researchers' gaze turned.

Steps toward AI

Meanwhile, Minsky had moved to the Massachusetts Institute of Technology in 1957, serving as a professor of mathematics there

OTHER SCIENTISTS: SEYMOUR PAPERT (1928–)

South African–born Seymour Papert arrived at MIT in 1963, and coauthored the definitive book *Perceptrons* with Marvin Minsky. Papert had a particular interest in how humans—particularly children—formed concepts and mastered skills. Papert was influenced by the work of Jean Piaget, a Swiss psychologist and educator. Piaget had found that contrary to what most educators believed, children did not think like "defective" or incomplete adults. Rather, children at each stage of their development had characteristic forms of reasoning.

Like Piaget, Papert believed that children developed good reasoning skills by being allowed to exercise them freely and learn from their mistakes. This idea, which became known as constructivism, again challenged educational orthodoxy, which believed that mistakes should be corrected immediately.

Papert began working with children at the MIT AI Lab and developed the LOGO computer language. Based on John McCarthy's Lisp, LOGO retained that language's flexibility and power but had simpler syntax. Further, LOGO was visual and interactive, allowing children to control a real or virtual "turtle" with commands and immediately see the result.

Papert demonstrated that students of all ages could understand computer science and mathematical concepts previously taught only to college students and programmers. Papert later became a wider-ranging educational activist who believes in transforming schools into real learning environments that encourage mastery through interaction and exploration.

from 1958 to 1961, later switching to the electrical engineering department. During the same time, Minsky and John McCarthy established Project MAC, MIT's first AI laboratory. In 1970, Minsky and McCarthy founded the MIT Artificial Intelligence Laboratory.

By the beginning of the 1960s the heady early years of artificial intelligence had ended. There were fascinating demonstrations of chess playing, theorem proving, and natural language processing programs, but most researchers had become less optimistic about being able to create a machine with an undeniable general-purpose intelligence.

Looking back, Minsky's 1961 paper "Steps toward Artificial Intelligence" (included in the collection *Computers and Thought*) reveals a remarkable catalogue of techniques that had been developed

---

SOLVING PROBLEMS: BASIC AI STRATEGIES

In his 1961 paper "Steps toward Artificial Intelligence" Marvin Minsky outlined basic features of AI programs that still form the basis of artificial problem solving today. These included searching and pattern-recognition techniques.

Searching is a common computer activity, familiar to anyone who has used Google or a database system. In AI, search techniques are needed for checking a large number of relevant items, such as mathematical theorems or chess moves. Because considering all possibilities or permutations is impossible even for today's computers, methods must be found for evaluating whether the current item is getting the program closer to or farther from a solution to the problem. This can be very difficult, because something that appears to be an improvement may be better only in a limited context.

Another way to focus a search is by pattern recognition, which makes searching much more efficient by identifying items likely to be relevant and not wasting time on the others. This requires identifying common characteristics of the desired items or finding something that remains "invariant" (the same) regardless of its position or orientation.

Learning techniques apply the results of previous problems to further narrowing the search for relevant items. There are many relevant learning strategies, which include being able to gauge how similar the current problem is to one that has already been solved and reinforcing correct guesses (as in a neural network).

Most people who have undertaken any sort of complicated project know how to identify intermediate goals on the way to the complete solution. It is often useful to break down a problem into "subproblems" (which again, might be similar to previously encountered ones) and then decide what method is to be applied to the subproblem.

in less than a decade's worth of research. These include not only basic forms of search, evaluation, and learning, but also the beginnings of a model of intelligence and a way that programs could begin to "understand" their own behavior. Minsky ended the paper with a look toward a future where time-sharing and multiprocessing programs would provide easier access to a growing amount of computing power.

Frames to Organize Knowledge

During the 1960s Minsky and many other researchers turned to robotics as an important area of AI research. Robots offered the possibility of reproducing intelligent, humanlike behavior through interaction between a machine and its environment. To do so, however, Minsky, like McCarthy, believed that the robot (or computer program) needed some way to organize knowledge and build a model of the world.

In response, Minsky developed the concept of frames, which he introduced in his 1974 paper "A Framework for the Representation

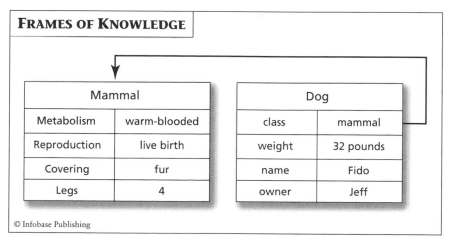

Frames organize the characteristics or properties of objects and also relate objects to one another.

of Knowledge." Frames are a way to categorize knowledge about the world, such as how to plan a trip. Frames can be broken into sub-frames. For example, a trip-planning frame might have subframes about air transportation, hotel reservations, and packing. Frames essentially tell a person (or a machine) how to "use" the world to accomplish things. Minsky's frames concept became a key to the construction of expert systems that today allow computers to advise on such topics as drilling for oil or medical diagnosis. (This field is often called knowledge engineering.)

In the 1970s Minsky and his colleagues at MIT designed robotic systems to test the ability to use frames to accomplish simpler tasks, such as navigating around the furniture in a room. The difficult challenge of giving a robot vision (the ability not only to perceive

Harold Cohen's AARON program also uses structured knowledge to develop its skills. The program creates original drawings and paintings (using real paint) based on a repertoire of artistic styles.

but also to "understand" the features of its environment) would also absorb much of their attention.

Although he is primarily an academic, Minsky also become involved in business ventures. He and Seymour Papert founded Logo Computer Systems, Inc. to create products based upon the easy-to-use but versatile LOGO language. In the early 1980s, Minsky established Thinking Machines Corporation, which built powerful computers that used as many as 64,000 processors working together.

Many Minds

Minsky continued to move fluidly between the worlds of the biological and the mechanical. He came to believe that the results of research into simulating cognitive behavior had fruitful implications for human psychology. In 1986, Minsky published *The Society of Mind*. This book suggests that the human mind is not a single entity (as classical psychology suggests) or a system with a small number of often-warring subentities (as psychoanalysis asserted).

It is more useful, Minsky suggests, to think of the mind as consisting of a multitude of independent agents that deal with different parts of the task of living and interact with one another in complex ways. The agents organize their efforts along what Minsky calls "K-lines" or "knowledge lines." Further, Minsky has suggested that what people call mind, or consciousness, or a sense of self may be what emerges from this ongoing interaction. Minsky suggested that, "you can build a mind from many little parts, each mindless by itself."

In his essay "Will Robots Inherit the Earth?" in *Understanding AI*, Minsky revisits and explains how a multiple-agent approach gives people a robust problem-solving ability:

In order to think effectively, you need multiple processes to help you describe, predict, explain, abstract and plan what your mind should do next. The reason we can think so well is not because we house mysterious sparklike talents and gifts but because we employ societies of agencies that work in concert to keep us from getting stuck. When

*we discover how these societies work, we can put them inside comput-
ers, too. Then if one procedure in a program gets stuck, another might
suggest an alternative approach. If you saw a machine do things like
that, you would certainly think it was conscious.*

Still Going Strong

Since 1990 Minsky has continued his research at MIT, exploring
the connections between biology, psychology, and the creations of
AI research. One area that intrigued him was the possibility of link-
ing humans to robots so that the human could see and interact with
the environment through the robot. This process, for which Minsky
coined the word "telepresence," is already used in a number of applications today, such as the use of robots by police or the military to
work in dangerous areas under the guidance of a remote operator,
and the use of surgical robots in medicine.

As he approaches 80 years of age in 2007, the still intellectually
and physically vigorous Marvin Minsky revels in provocative insight
and challenging the "AI establishment" that he helped create. In his
essay "Marvin Minsky: The Mastermind of Artificial Intelligence"
in *Understanding AI,* John Horgan reflects on his approach to interviewing Minsky back in the early 1990s:

> *. . . the same traits that made Minsky a successful pioneer of AI have
> led him to become increasingly alienated from the field as it matures.
> Before my meeting with Minsky, in fact, other AI workers warn me
> that he might be somewhat cranky; if I do not want the interview cut
> short, I should not ask him too directly about the current slump in AI
> or what some workers characterize as his own waning influence in the
> field. One prominent theorist pleads with me not to take advantage of
> Minsky's penchant for hyperbole. "Ask him if he means it, and if he
> doesn't say it three times, you shouldn't use it," the theorist urges.*

Horgan goes on to paint a description of one of two of AI's
"elder statesmen" (the other being Minsky's longtime colleague John
McCarthy):

Solving Problems: Improving or Copying the Brain?

In the Scientific American book *Understanding AI* Minsky explains how techniques from advanced neuroscience will enable considerable improvement in the functioning of the human brain—perhaps even immortality.

> The more we learn about our brains, the more ways we will find to improve them. Each brain has hundreds of specialized regions. We know only a little about what each one does or how it does it, but as soon as we find out how any one part works, researchers will try to devise ways to extend that part's capacity . . . With further advances, no part of the brain will be out-of-bounds for attaching new accessories. In the end, we will find ways to replace every part of the body and brain and thus repair all the defects and injuries that make our lives so brief.

Probably the most ambitious project in AI is the replication of the human brain or its functional equivalent. In his essay "Will Robots Inherit the Earth?" in *Understanding AI,* Minsky describes the challenge as follows:

> To make a replacement of a human brain, we would need to know something about how each of the synapses [nerve connections] relates to the two cells it joins. We would also have to know how each of those structures responds to the various electric fields, hormones, neurotransmitters, nutrients and other chemicals that are active in its neighborhood. A human brain contains trillions of synapses, so this is no small requirement.

Today's scanning technology is providing increasingly detailed "maps" of the brain, down to the level of the neuronal connections themselves. However, critics of brain replication point to the 100 trillion or so of potential connections involved, dwarfing the complexity of even the largest of today's computers. Minsky suggests, however, that

> . . . we would not need to know every minute detail . . . [to] copy a functional brain it should suffice to replicate just enough of the function of each part to produce its important effect on other parts.

Even [Minsky's] physical appearance has an improvisational air. His large, round head seems entirely bald but is actually fringed by hairs as transparent as optical fibers. He wears a crocheted belt that supports, in addition to his pants, a belly pack and a holster containing pliers with retractable jaws. With his paunch and vaguely Asian features, he resembles a high-tech Buddha.

Colleague Roger Schank said to interviewer John Brockman in 1998 that

Marvin Minsky is the smartest person I've ever known. He's absolutely full of ideas, and he hasn't gotten one step slower or one step dumber. One of the things about Marvin that's really fantastic is that he never gets too old. He's wonderfully childlike. I think that's a major factor explaining why he's such a good thinker.

The Emotion Machine

Minsky's latest book is called *The Emotion Machine*. In it he suggests that it is a mistake to consider thinking and emotion to be different things. Rather, as he says in the Brockman interview,

. . . emotions are not alternatives to thinking; they are simply different types of thinking. I regard each emotional state to be a different arrangement or disposition of mental resources. Each uses some different combination of techniques or strategies for thinking. Thus such emotions as fear, hunger, or pain are the result of the mind prioritizing danger, food, or physical distress respectively.

Minsky explained to writer R. Colin Johnson that "the big feature of human-level intelligence is not what it does when it works but what it does when it's stuck." He believes the mind organizes knowledge into "scripts" that can be adapted on the fly. When a new situation arises, the mind looks for ways in which

ISSUES: MINSKY ON AI RESEARCH AND THE NATURE OF CONSCIOUSNESS

In his interview with Horgan, Minsky also took the opportunity to describe some of his longstanding misgivings about today's AI research. He suggests that "If AI has not progressed as far as it should have, that is because modern researchers have succumbed to 'physics envy'—the desire to reduce the intricacies of the brain to simple formulae." (This echoes an old adage: make things simple, but not *too* simple.)

Minsky also cites "the dreaded investment principle in which [researchers] are defining smaller and smaller subspecialities that they examine in more detail, but they're not open to doing things in a different way." Minsky noted to writer Kevin Featherly in 2001 that few researchers seem willing to tackle the work of getting a computer to understand and use "common sense":

What happens is that people try that, and then they read something about neural nets and say, 'Maybe if we make a baby learning machine and just expose it to a lot, it'll get smarter. Or maybe we'll make a genetic algorithm and try to re-evolve it, or maybe we'll use mathematical logic.' There are about 10 fads. And the fads have eaten up everybody.

Part of the resistance to the common sense approach may be the belief that there is something about human consciousness that simply cannot be replicated by a computer program, no matter how much knowledge is fed to it. But in a typically provocative statement in the Horgan interview Minsky insists that "The mystery of consciousness is 'trivial.' I've solved it, and I don't understand why people don't listen." In the Brockman interview he calls "consciousness" a "suitcase of methods that we use for thinking about our own minds." Minsky goes on to suggest that in his "society of mind" the experience we call consciousness may be the product of one of the "agents" whose job it is to remember or record what the other parts are doing. And recording data is something that computers are already good at.

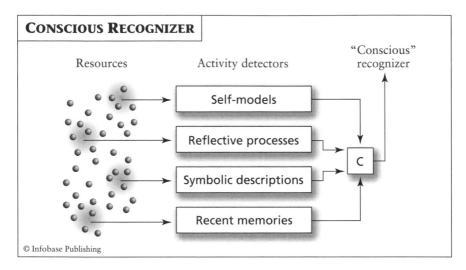

In Marvin Minsky's theory of the mind, consciousness results from a compo-nent or agent that recognizes and tracks the flow of processing where memories, descriptions, and reflections are used to create models of the self.

it is similar or analogous to a plan or procedure that has worked in the past.

The book will also explore how people (and animals) acquire new goals through attachment to parents or other objects of love. (Here Minsky gives an approving nod to Freud, suggesting a similarity between the information-processing ideas of computer science and the mental processes identified by psychoanalysts.)

Minsky's wide-ranging interests have also included music composi-tion (he designed a music synthesizer). He has written science fiction (the *Turing Option,* coauthored with Harry Harrison in 1992). The house where he and his wife Gloria (a pediatrician) live is filled with Minsky's unusual inventions and hidden features, including a mechani-cal arm that mathematically integrates its 36 pulleys and six joints.

Minsky's less tangible but perhaps more important legacy includes the mentoring of nearly two generations of students in AI and robot-ics, as well as his seeking greater public support for AI research and computer science.

Minsky has received numerous awards, including the ACM Turing Award (1969), the Japan Prize (1990), and the International Joint Conference on Artificial Intelligence Research Excellence Award (1991).

Chronology

1927	Marvin Minsky is born on August 9 in New York City
1945–1946	Minsky serves as an electronics technician in the U.S. Navy
1950	Minsky receives a B.A. in mathematics from Harvard
1954	Minsky receives his doctorate in mathematics
1956	The Dartmouth summer conference on AI brings together Minsky, John McCarthy, and other key researchers
1957	Minsky becomes a professor of mathematics at MIT.
1959	Minsky and John McCarthy found the MIT Artificial Intelligence Project (Project MAC, later the MIT AI Laboratory).
1960s	Minsky directs the MIT AI Lab from 1964 to 1973; he works on knowledge representation in "frames"
1970s	Minsky applies frames theory to helping robots "understand" and navigate through their environment
1980s	Minsky founds Thinking Machines Corporation to market multiprocessor computers
1986	Minsky's book *Society of Mind* offers a theory of multiple "agents" or cooperating intelligences
1990s	Minsky continues research at MIT, including remote links between humans and computers or robots
2000s	Minsky's latest work explores the relationship between goals, planning, attachment, and emotion in human life
2006	Minsky publishes *The Emotion Machine*

Further Reading

Books

Editors of *Scientific American. Understanding Artificial Intelligence.* New York: Warner Books, 2002. (Also available as an "eBook").
> Includes introductory essays on major aspects of AI as well as an interview with Marvin Minsky.

McCorduck, Pamela. *Machines Who Think.* 2nd ed. Natick, Mass.: A. K. Peters, 2004.
> Describes much of Minsky's work and the milieu of early AI research.

Minsky, Marvin. *The Emotion Machine: Commonsense Thinking, Artificial Intelligence, and the Future of the Human Mind.* New York: Simon & Schuster, 2006.
> Develops a new theory of mental processes, emotions, and "attachments" in the development of the mind.

———. *The Society of Mind.* New York: Simon & Schuster, 1986.
> An eclectic mosaic of a book that introduced Minsky's intriguing theory of multiple agents cooperating to create the experience of "mind."

Articles

Brockman, John. "Consciousness Is a Big Suitcase: A Talk with Marvin Minsky." Available online. URL: http://www.edge.org/3rd_culture/minsky/index.html. Accessed on August 15, 2006.
> Minsky provides a clear explanation of his theory of multiple agent minds and suggests avoiding "suitcase words" that obscure rather than explain mental processes.

Featherly, Kevin. "AI Pioneer Minsky: Machines Must Use Their Common Sense." *Newsbytes,* 31 August 2001, p. NWSB01244003.
> Minsky discusses where he believes AI research is going wrong and pans the Steven Spielberg film *AI.*

Johnson, R. Colin. "A Veritable Cognitive Mind—For MIT's Minsky, Practical AI Is a Matter of Common Sense." *Electronic Engineering Times,* 28 July 2003, p. 19.
> Briefly previews Minsky's ideas on human cognition from his forthcoming book.

Minsky, Marvin. "Memoir on Inventing the Confocal Scanning Microscope." *Scanning,* vol. 10, 1988, pp. 128–138. Available online. URL: http://web.media.mit.edu/~minsky/papers/ ConfocalMemoir.html. Accessed on September 22, 2006.
Minsky describes the background of his interest in optics and how he invented and patented a new type of microscope.

Web Sites

"Marvin Minsky." [Home page] MIY Media Lab. Available online. URL: http://web.media.mit.edu/~minsky. Accessed on August 15, 2006.
Includes a selection of Minsky's writings, including a draft of his book *The Emotion Machine.*

5

HARNESSING KNOWLEDGE

EDWARD FEIGENBAUM AND EXPERT SYSTEMS

There are many compelling projects in AI research. In its first decade researchers had created programs that could make deductions and prove theorems, understand simple "plain English" instructions, recognize patterns, and even learn from experience. In their different ways John McCarthy and Marvin Minsky had pursued new ways to represent and manipulate knowledge. They and others repeatedly suggested that one of the most important and useful projects would be to find a way that a program could systematically take facts and rules about some field and draw conclusions or make decisions based on them. Edward Feigenbaum would do this by developing the "expert system," a program that could take a "knowledge base" of assertions and perform tasks ranging from chemical analysis to medical diagnosis and airline scheduling.

Edward Feigenbaum was born on January 20, 1936, in Weehawken, New Jersey. His father, a Polish immigrant, died before Feigenbaum's first birthday. Feigenbaum's stepfather, an accountant and bakery manager, was fascinated by science and regularly brought the boy to the Hayden Planetarium's shows and to every department of the vast Museum of Natural History. The electromechanical Monroe calculator his father used to keep accounts at the bakery particularly fascinated young Feigenbaum.

A "Practical" Career

Feigenbaum's interest in science collided to a certain extent with the practical concerns of parents for whom the Great Depression of the 1930s was still a vivid memory. As he explains to Dennis Shasha and Cathy Lazere in *Out of Their Minds*, Feigenbaum reached a sort of compromise:

There was enough attention paid during my young life to getting enough money for day-to-day living. Engineering seemed a more satisfactory alternative than science—more practical, more money.

Electrical engineering was at the intersection point between science and mathematics. Everything in electrical engineering was relatively abstract. Whereas mechanical or civil engineering was the real stuff. I was never much of a "stuff" person. I'm more of a "thoughts" person.

Edward Feigenbaum developed expert systems, knowledge-driven programs that have mastered tasks ranging from medical diagnosis to airline scheduling. (Edward Feigenbaum)

More or less accepting that practical logic, Feigenbaum entered the Carnegie Institute of Technology (now Carnegie Mellon University) as an electrical engineering student. Fortunately for a "thoughts" person, a professor encouraged him to look at courses outside the normal electrical engineering curriculum.

Feigenbaum began to take courses at Carnegie's recently established Graduate School of Industrial Administration. There he encountered John von Neumann's game theory and was fascinated by the way in which mathematics could be applied not just to physical matters like electrical conductivity but also to social interactions.

Meeting the "Thinking Machine"

Even more fruitful was Feigenbaum's encounter with Herbert Simon and Allen Newell, who were developing the first computer models of human thinking and decision making (see chapter 2, "Mind in a Box"). As recounted by Shasha and Lazere, Feigenbaum remembers that when Newell announced their development of a "thinking machine" and passed out computer manuals to the class:

> *I took the manual home with me and read it straight through the night. When the next day broke, I was a born again—you can't say "computer scientist" because there was no such thing as a computer scientist at the time. Anyway, I realized what I wanted to do. So the next thing was, how to do that?*

Feigenbaum decided to follow Newell's and Simon's lead and write a computer simulation of a human mental process. Instead of decision making, however, Feigenbaum chose the somewhat simpler (but still important) process of memorization. The result was the Elementary Perceiver and Memorizer (EPAM). The program modeled the way people memorize new words by noticing how they are similar to or different from other words. For example, one might, having learned that AI is an acronym for "artificial intelligence," later encounter AL, meaning "artificial life." Both terms have artificiality in common. Feigenbaum created a structure he called a "discrimination net" to allow a computer to be "trained" to make such distinctions.

Feigenbaum's program was an important contribution to AI. Its "discrimination net," which attempted to distinguish between different stimuli by retaining key bits of information, would eventually become part of the research on neural networks (see chapter 4, "Simulated Brains").

From Deduction to Induction

Together with Julian Feldman, Feigenbaum edited the 1962 book *Computers and Thought*, which summarized both the remarkable progress and perplexing difficulties encountered during the AI field's first decade. Feigenbaum's own contribution to the book, a paper titled "The Simulation of Verbal Learning Behavior" describes EPAM and stresses that it is a program that focuses on a psychological process, not a neurological one, and that it is about information processing, not how parts of the brain are connected.

In his foreword to the book, Feigenbaum advocates a new direction in AI research:

Artificial intelligence has been concerned with deductive kinds of things—proving theorems, making moves in chess. How about the process of empirical induction where we go from a wide variety of data to a generalization or a hypothesis about what that data means?

Feigenbaum spent the early 1960s trying to come up with a concrete application for an inductive program. Working on a project to develop a mass spectrometer for a Mars probe's search for life on the red planet, Feigenbaum and his fellow researchers became frustrated at the computer's lack of knowledge about basic rules of chemistry. Feigenbaum then decided that such rules might be encoded in a "knowledge base" in such a way that the program could apply it to the data being gathered from chemical samples.

A Stanford colleague, Nobel Prize–winning geneticist Joshua Lederberg, suggested a project: Develop a program that can analyze the data from a mass spectrograph to determine the actual molecular structure of the substance in question. As Feigenbaum noted to Pamela McCorduck:

It was a problem that had all the elements of classical empirical induction. Here's an array of data that comes from a physical instrument, the mass spectrograph. Here's a set of primitive constructs out of which to compose a hypothesis about what organic compound is being analyzed. Here's a legal move-generator for generating all possible hypotheses. The problem is . . . how do you find the good ones? And how do you employ knowledge of the world of chemistry, mass spectrometry, to constrain [limit] the set of alternatives, steering away from large sets of unfruitful ones?

In a way, the problem was similar to the challenge to early AI researchers: How do you get a computer to play decent (if not brilliant) chess moves? The difference is that while the universe of chess moves is very large, one can "code in" some general principles for evaluating moves, check for captures, evaluate positional features, and so on. In biochemistry, however, there were not only general principles but also many specific rules about structure. To generate good hypotheses or "moves" in that game, the program would have to access systematically a growing body of structured knowledge.

An Automated Chemist

The result of the work of Feigenbaum and colleague Robert K. Lindsay was the 1965 program DENDRAL, the first of what would become a host of successful and productive programs known as expert systems. A further advance came in 1970 with META-DENDRAL, a program that could not only apply existing rules to determine the structure of a compound, it could also compare known structures with the existing database of rules and infer new rules, thus improving DENDRAL's performance. (If one thinks of DENDRAL as an automated lab assistant, META-DENDRAL is more like an automated research scientist.)

In his online article "The Age of Intelligent Machines" Feigenbaum points out:

> *What emerged from the many experiments with DENDRAL was an empirical hypothesis that the source of the program's power to figure out chemical structures from spectral data was its knowledge of . . . chemistry. For DENDRAL, knowledge was power. . . . But the prevailing view in AI at the time ascribed power to the reasoning powers [of the program] . . . not the knowledge base.*

The AI world gave DENDRAL and its successors mixed reviews. Some AI researchers assumed that the program was so specialized in its application to chemistry that they could learn little from it. Others acknowledged the program's usefulness but assumed it was too "mechanical" in its operation to be interesting as a form of artificial intelligence.

The Priority of Knowledge

Feigenbaum did not shy away from such criticisms. Indeed he went on to formulate what he calls the Knowledge Principle, which says that

> *reasoning processes of an intelligent system, being general and therefore weak, are not the source of power that leads to high levels of competence in behavior. . . . If a program is to perform well, it must know a great deal about the world in which it operates. In the absence of knowledge, reasoning won't help.*

Shasha and Lazere quote Feigenbaum giving a pithy example of the priority of knowledge over generalized reasoning:

> *Suppose we are in Georgetown [Washington, D.C.]. Georgetown has a great medical school. It also has an excellent math department. So we are sitting here and one of us gets sick—has a heart attack or something. We rush that person over to the hospital where there are people trained in medicine. We don't rush them over to the math department where there are excellent reasoners. Right? Because reasoning doesn't make any difference. You need to know about medicine, not about reasoning.*

(Of course this is overstated for effect. One needs both specific knowledge and the capacity to generalize and reason about the unknown. As described later, Feigenbaum sees these capabilities gradually being built upon the foundation of solid knowledge-based systems.)

This shift from reasoning to knowledge was an interesting development. Most AI researchers still seemed to be seeking an ever-deeper understanding of how reasoning (both human and artificial) worked. They wanted to create and test models. However, by the late 1970s, DENDRAL was joined by a host of other programs that used a knowledge base and a component called an inference engine that could create a chain of logic in order to answer a query.

Two of these programs were in the medical field. MYCIN (developed at Stanford) acted as a consultant for specialists in infectious diseases. Although its backward-chaining logic was simple, the program was noted for its ability to interact with its medical users and even explain how it came up with a given diagnosis. Another medical expert system was Internist, an electronic "doctor" that had a knowledge base of 572 diseases and 4,500 manifestations or symptoms.

Building an Expert System

To create an expert system, one first carefully interviews the expert(s) and gets them to express their knowledge in terms of rules or probabilities. For example, suppose one were writing a computer baseball simulation. One might interview some real big league baseball managers and ask questions like "When do you call for the batter to sacrifice to move the runner to second base?" This knowledge is then encoded into rules ranging from the obvious (if there are already two outs, the batter can't sacrifice) to the more arcane (if you are at Coors Field where the ball flies higher in thinner air and leads to high scoring games, playing for only one run is usually not advised). Rules can also be expressed in terms of probabilities or "fuzzy logic" where instead of a single conclusion the result might be true 80 percent of the time. The result of all these assertions is called a knowledge base.

The other part of the system is called the inference engine. It follows the links in the knowledge base, often according to IF-THEN rules. Using the baseball example, such a rule might be:

IF *there are two outs* THEN *batter must swing away*

Or, a probability might be used:

IF *there are two outs* AND *the batter is a fast runner*
THEN *batter may try to bunt for a hit (20 percent chance)*

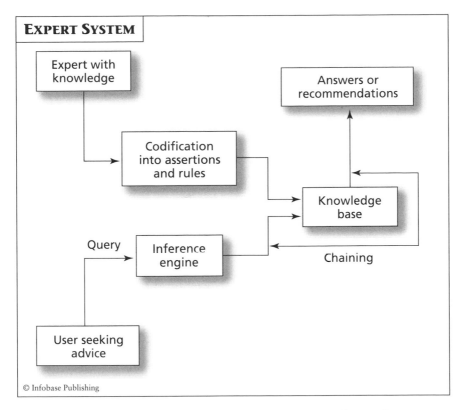

An expert system links a user to a knowledge base by way of an "inference engine" that can search for appropriate rules and draw conclusions to answer his or her question.

In addition to working its way through the knowledge base, an expert system can also contain stored procedures that it calls as necessary. For example, an expert system in charge of determining the best combination of shipping cost and speed for a business might call a procedure to check online with Federal Express or UPS to see if their rates have changed, or consult a calendar to see whether holidays might affect the arrival time of a package. The expert system can also use procedures to get information from the person asking the question, such as "Does your package have to arrive: a) tomorrow morning b) sometime tomorrow or c) sometime in the next two days?"

An important feature of expert systems is that they are modular. In many cases there is no need to build a new system from scratch for each application. Instead, one can buy an "expert system shell" that includes the inference engine and a set of tools for building the knowledge base. By working with the appropriate human experts, the same shell might be used to develop an expert system for planning weddings or to create a system for helping real estate agents decide which houses to show to a given buyer. Of course some systems may be so complex or unusual that they require creating customized forms or rules and procedures.

The "Expert Company"

Unlike abstract experimental reasoning programs, expert systems offered the possibility of actually making good money solving real-world problems. By the late 1970s, besides being used in the medical field, expert systems were being used in industry (engineering, manufacturing, and maintenance), science (molecular biology and geology), and even in military signal processing. Today expert systems are used by airlines to schedule the most efficient routing of planes to airports to deal with anticipated problems with weather, airport congestion, or mechanical difficulties. Other expert systems help air traffic controllers recognize potential collisions.

During the 1980s Feigenbaum coedited the four-volume *Handbook of Artificial Intelligence*. He also introduced expert systems to a lay audience in two books, *The Fifth Generation* (coauthored with Pamela McCorduck) and *The Rise of the Expert Company*.

Feigenbaum combined scientific creativity with entrepreneurship in founding a company called IntelliGenetics and serving as a director of Teknowledge and IntelliCorp. These companies pioneered the commercialization of expert systems. In doing so, Feigenbaum and his colleagues firmly established the discipline of "knowledge engineering"—the capturing and encoding of professional knowledge in medicine, chemistry, engineering, and other fields so that it can be used by an expert system.

In reality, just as life continues below ground in a snowy field, AI research also continued. Sometimes it "disguised" itself under

CONNECTIONS: PROLOG, THE LOGIC PROGRAMMING LANGUAGE

It is difficult to construct knowledge bases and inference engines with conventional programming languages. Languages such as ALGOL are based on defining data and procedures for working with that data. Such languages have no basic structures for encoding logical relationships.

In 1972, Alain Colmerauer, a French researcher, and Robert Kowalski of Edinburgh University in Scotland created Prolog, short for "Programming in Logic"). In Prolog, it is easy to state relationships between objects. For example, the fact that Joe is the father of Bill would be written as:

Father (Joe, Bill).

The programmer then defines logical rules that apply to the facts. For example:

father (X, Y) :- parent (X, Y), is male (X)

grandfather (X, Y) :- father (X, Z), parent (Z, Y)

The first rule states that a person X is the father of a person Y if he is the parent of Y and is male. The second rule says that X is Y's grandfather if he is the father of a person Z who in turn is a parent of Y.

When a Prolog program runs, it processes queries, or assertions whose truth is to be examined. Using a process called unification, the Prolog system searches for facts or rules that apply to the query and then attempts to create a logical chain leading to proving the query is true. If the chain breaks (because no matching fact or rule can be found), the system "backtracks" by looking for another matching fact or rule from which to attempt another chain.

Prolog became widely used in the late 1970s and 1980s, spurred on by the Japanese decision to use it for their massive Fifth Generation Computer program. Although this attempt to build a new type of super logic computer ultimately failed, Prolog continues to be used in a number of areas of artificial intelligence research, particularly the construction of expert systems.

ISSUES: THE "AI WINTER"

By the 1980s expert systems were by far the most commercially successful AI applications. However, just as this practical version of AI was proving its success in many fields, the traditional research into such things as reasoning and natural language seemed to be in decline. The criticism of neural networks (see chapter 4, "Simulated Brains") by Marvin Minsky and Seymour Papert suggested that this once-promising technique would hit a dead end.

On a broader scale, the extravagant promises of some AI research-ers that such things as automatic language translation and personal robot assistants were just around the corner were proving to be a far cry from reality.

Symptoms of the "freeze" coming over the field could be seen in several areas. Government funding of AI projects was cut sharply, particularly the DARPA (Defense Advanced Research Projects Agency) money that had been so important since the 1950s. Many companies marketing special-purpose hardware for AI (such as "Lisp machines") failed, although many observers suggest the real culprit was the coming of more powerful desktop computers to replace scientific workstations. Even the capabilities of expert systems were oversold to investors, just as the Web would be overhyped in the late 1990s.

another name, such as "knowledge-based systems." Sometimes it morphed, finding its way into "smarter" consumer products, enter-taining robot toys, and, in recent years, on the Internet in the form of "intelligent" search engines and agents that can create customized news pages. As with the Internet "dot-bust" of the early 2000s, "AI winters" are probably part of a natural cycle arising from promising research creating a ferment of new investments, which eventually must be winnowed down to genuinely viable applications.

What Comes Next?

In "The Age of Intelligent Machines" Feigenbaum both praises the many successes of knowledge-based systems in a variety of fields and acknowledges that much remains to be done. Along with many other AI researchers over the past decades, Feigenbaum points out that programs would be easier to use and more helpful if they could understand natural language with its use of synonyms, expressions, and even metaphors.

Feigenbaum also discusses recent research in developing systems that can fall back on generalized knowledge when no specific facts are found in the knowledge base. For example, a knowledge-based CAD (Computer-assisted Design) program might have internal models of electronics, metallurgy, and physics. If it cannot find a particular circuit component in its database the system can look for ways to achieve the desired characteristics using some combination of components.

Another strategy that could make knowledge-based systems more robust is for them to understand and use analogies. To do so, the

The "Connection Machine" can combine the power of hundreds of separate computer processors. A special kind of programming must be used to coordinate them. (NASA)

program must be able to reason about both the similarities and differences between two objects. Thus if the knowledge base of some future "nanny" robot says that it is dangerous to let the children wander into the street, it might also conclude that the family dog (which is also small and soft compared to big, heavy, fast-moving cars) should be similarly confined.

Looking further into the future, Feigenbaum quotes Marvin Minksy: "Can you imagine that they used to have libraries where the books didn't talk to each other?" In other words, in the future knowledge will be active, not passive. It will not wait to be discovered but will communicate itself to interested agents, both human and computer, that will work collaboratively. Feigenbaum calls such a future library a "knowledge server." Just as a file server in a computer network today makes files or documents available from a central location while keeping them organized, a knowledge server can

collect relevant information; it can summarize; it can pursue relationships. It acts as a consultant on specific problems, offering advice on particular solutions, justifying those solutions with citations or with a fabric of general reasoning. If the user can suggest a solution or a hypothesis, it can check this and even suggest extensions. Or it can critique the user viewpoint with a detailed rationale of its agreement or disagreement.

Remaining active in the 1990s, Feigenbaum was the second president of the American Association for Artificial Intelligence and (from 1994 to 1997) chief scientist of the U.S. Air Force. He contributed his expertise by serving on the board of many influential research organizations, including the Computer Science Advisory Board of the National Science Foundation and the National Research Council's Computer Science and Technology Board. The World Congress of Expert Systems created the Feigenbaum Medal in his honor, making him its first recipient in 1991. In 1995, Feigenbaum received the prestigious Association for Computing Machinery's A. M. Turing Award together with Raj Reddy, "For pioneering the design and construction of large-

PARALLELS: JAPAN'S "FIFTH GENERATION"

In 1982, Japan's Ministry of International Trade and Industry announced a major initiative to create a "fifth generation computer." (The first four generations were vacuum tubes, transistors, integrated circuits, and microprocessors). The hardware was to feature "massive parallelism" or the use of many processors working together. The most interesting aspect of the project, however, was to be the integration of artificial intelligence software into the system. All data in the computer would be organized in the form of knowledge bases rather than ordinary files. An inference engine and a logic-programming language (Prolog) would combine to allow for the creation of powerful expert systems and other applications.

The announcement of the Fifth Generation project stirred interest and some alarm in the American computer industry. After all, Japan had already showed its leadership in automotive manufacturing and consumer electronics. Similar projects were soon started in the United States, Great Britain, and Europe in order to head off the competitive threat.

By the end of the decade, however, the Japanese Fifth Generation project had petered out. The rapid growth of power of single-processor desktop computers (and the use of networking) made multiprocessor computers less attractive. Meanwhile, Prolog had to be abandoned in favor of developing a concurrent (parallel programming) language that could coordinate multiple processes and processors. Finally, the growing use of the Internet and data-mining techniques became an easier alternative for processing knowledge for most applications. The project was officially abandoned in 1993, a victim of technical difficulties and bad timing.

scale artificial intelligence systems, demonstrating the practical importance and potential commercial impact of artificial intelligence technology."

Today Feigenbaum is director of the Knowledge Systems Laboratory, a division of the Stanford University Artificial Intelligence Laboratory.

Chronology

1936	Edward Feigenbaum is born on January 20 in Weehawken, New Jersey
1952	Feigenbaum enters Carnegie as an engineering student, encounters Newell and Simon and their "thinking" computer program
1957	Feigenbaum develops EPAM, a program that simulates human memory and discrimination
1962	Feigenbaum and Julian Feldman edit the seminal book *Computers and Thought*
1965	The program DENDRAL demonstrates knowledge-based reasoning in analyzing molecules
1970	The program META-DENDRAL is able to infer new rules to apply to future problems
1972	The Prolog language makes it easier to build expert systems
1970s	Expert systems begin to appear in a variety of fields. An example is MYCIN, which can diagnose certain types of infections
1980s	Expert systems become a major part of the software industry The Japanese attempt to build a new generation of computers based on logic programming
1995	Feigenbaum and Raj Reddy jointly win the ACM Turing Award for pioneering achievements in AI

Further Reading

Books

Feigenbaum, Edward, Julian Feldman, and Paul Armer, eds. *Computers and Thought*. Cambridge, Mass.: MIT Press, 1995.
 A classic collection of papers on different aspects of AI.
Feigenbaum, Edward, Pamela McCorduck, and H. Penny Nii. *The Rise of the Expert Company: How Visionary Companies Are*

Using Artificial Intelligence to Achieve Higher Productivity and Profits. New York: Vintage Books, 1989.

Describes a number of actual business applications of expert systems as of the late 1980s; useful today as a historical overview.

Shasha, Dennis, and Cathy Lazere. *Out of Their Minds: The Lives and Discoveries of 15 Great Computer Scientists.* New York: Copernicus, 1995.

Includes chapters on Feigenbaum, John McCarthy, and Douglas Lenat.

Articles

Feigenbaum, Edward. "The Age of Intelligent Machines: Knowledge Processing—From File Servers to Knowledge Servers." KurzweilAI. net. Available online. URL: http://www.kurzweilai.net/meme/frame. html?main=/articles/art0098.html. Accessed on August 16, 2006.

Reviews the development of AI and knowledge technology, arguing that the field is currently in a transition from data processing to knowledge processing.

"Introduction to Expert Systems." Expertise2Go. Available online. URL: http://www.expertise2go.com/webesie/tutorials/ESIntro. Accessed on August 16, 2006.

This tutorial presents expert system concepts using the example of an expert system that diagnoses car trouble, showing how an expert system models a good human consultant.

THE COMMONSENSE COMPUTER

DOUGLAS LENAT AND THE CYC PROJECT

By the 1980s a revolution in the automatic processing of knowledge was well under way. Several key ideas contributed to this revolution. Marvin Minsky's concept of frames provided one way to tell a computer program how the world worked, such as specifying the physical characteristics of objects or the ways in which people might use them. Thanks to the work of researchers such as Edward Feigenbaum, expert systems could draw on their knowledge bases to carry out complex tasks, often more quickly and accurately than human experts.

One goal still seemed to be out of reach, and it was the most ambitious and cherished goal of AI: the creation of a program that was not an expert but a generalist. That is, a program that could, like a human being, prove a geometry theorem in the morning, plan a vacation in the afternoon, and discuss the day's news or a bit of gossip at a dinner party. To function the way people do, such a system would need a knowledge base that amounted to an entire encyclopedia with hundreds of volumes. Douglas Lenat has set out to create just that.

Douglas Lenat was born in Philadelphia, Pennsylvania, on September 13, 1950, and he grew up in Wilmington, Delaware. His parents ran a soda-bottling business. Lenat became enthusiastic about science in sixth grade when he started reading Isaac Asimov's popular nonfiction books about biology and physics.

About that same time, however, Lenat's father died suddenly, and financial difficulties meant that the family had to move frequently. As a result, Lenat was constantly being enrolled in new schools. Each school would put him in the beginning rather than advanced "track" because they had not evaluated him, and he often had to repeat semesters. However, this constantly disrupted education may have strengthened Lenat for the coming challenges of his career. As he recalled to Dennis Shasha and Cathy Lazere:

Douglas Lenat has undertaken a decades-long project to create an encyclopedic knowledge base that could enable programs to understand many aspects of human life and the world. (Wundr Studio)

You constantly had to prove yourself instead of resting on context and circumstances. People in the good classes were expected to do well and didn't work very hard. The people in my classes were not expected to do well and you really had to work hard.

Saved by Science

Lenat turned to science projects as a way of breaking out of this intellectual ghetto. In 1967, his project about finding prime numbers got him into the finals in the International Science Fair in Detroit, Michigan. At the fair, he and other contestants were judged by working scientists and were treated like beginning scientists themselves. This experience confirmed Lenat's desire for a scientific career.

In 1968, Lenat enrolled in the University of Pennsylvania to study mathematics and physics, graduating in 1972 with bachelor's degrees in both disciplines plus a master's degree in applied math. (Because of his low number in the Vietnam draft lottery, Lenat felt he had to get as much education as he could while his student deferment lasted.)

However, Lenat became somewhat disenchanted with both disciplines. He didn't believe he could quite reach the top rank of mathematicians. As for physics, he found it to be too abstract and bogged down with its ever growing but incoherent collection of newly discovered particles.

Meanwhile, though, Lenat had became intrigued when he took an introductory course in artificial intelligence. Although the field was still very young ("like being back doing astronomy right after the invention of the telescope," he would say to Shasha and Lazere), it offered the possibility of "building something like a mental amplifier that would make you smarter, hence would enable you to do even more and better things." Finally, though, Lenat concluded that "it was clear that researchers in the field [of AI] didn't know what the hell they were doing."

A Commonsense Approach

At the time the most successful approach to practical AI had been rule-based or expert systems (see chapter 5, "A Little Knowledge"). These programs could solve mathematical problems or even analyze molecules. They did it by systematically applying sets of specific rules to a problem. But while this approach could be quite effective within narrow application areas, it did not capture the wide-ranging, versatile reasoning employed by human beings. AI researchers had ruefully noted that "It's easier to simulate a geologist than a five-year old." Human beings, even five-year-old ones, are equipped with a large fund of what we call common sense. Because of this, humans approaching a given situation already know a lot about what to do and what not to do.

Inspired by John McCarthy, who was trying to overcome such shortcomings, Lenat went to Stanford University for his doctorate, after first trying Caltech for a few months. Lenat had hoped to work with McCarthy, but the latter went on sabbatical. Lenat's adviser was Cordell Green, who had made considerable advances in what is known as "automatic programming." This is the attempt to set up a system that would accept a sufficiently rigorous description of a problem and then generate the program code needed to solve the problem.

As Lenat became more familiar with the AI field he began to take a more practical approach. As he noted to Shasha and Lazere:

> *Before Stanford I had seen myself as a formalist; Cordell (and my later mentors Feigenbaum and Buchanan) impressed upon me the value of being an empirical scientist even in an area like AI—looking at data, doing experiments, using the computer to do experiments to test falsifiable hypotheses.*

Hypotheses in computer science were harder to test than those in the physical sciences. A particle under certain conditions either behaves as predicted or it does not. The results of an AI project, however, are often far from clear. Nevertheless, one could focus on the performance of specific tasks and see whether in fact the computer can perform them.

The Automated Mathematician

Lenat became interested in applying the idea of automated reasoning to mathematics. (This was a long-standing topic in AI, going back to the logic and geometry theorem-proving programs of the mid-1950s.) For his doctoral thesis Lenat wrote a program called AM (Automated Mathematician). The program "thought" more like a human mathematician than earlier math programs had been able to do. It applied heuristics (a fancy term basically meaning "informed guesses") that experience had often shown to be fruitful. For example, since many mathematical operations produce interesting results with certain values such as zero and one, the program would try those values and draw conclusions if they yielded unusual results. Similarly, if several different techniques lead to the same result, the program would conclude that the result is more likely to be correct.

The AM program used 115 assertions or rules from set theory plus 243 heuristic rules. By exploring combinations of them, it was able to derive 300 mathematical concepts including such sophisticated ones as "every even number greater than three is the sum of two primes" (this was known to mathematicians as Goldbach's conjecture.) The program also discovered something similar to the work of the Indian mathematical genius Ramanujan concerning "highly composite" numbers that had many divisors. At the same time, the program failed to make certain discoveries that Lenat was expecting it to find, such as the different kinds of infinity found in the work of George Cantor.

The AM program intrigued a number of mathematicians as well as other computer scientists such as Donald Knuth, who were interested in what paths the program took or did not take, and what happened as it moved farther from its mathematical moorings. After awhile, though, AM seemed to run out of ideas though it continued to search fruitlessly.

After receiving his Ph.D. in 1976 Lenat became an assistant professor at Carnegie Mellon University for two years and then returned to Stanford. He continued to explore the use of heuristics in programs. His new program, Eurisko, was an attempt to generalize the heuristic reasoning that had been surprisingly successful (at least at first) with AM, and to allow the program not only to apply various heuristics but also to formulate and test new ones. Eurisko turned out to have some interesting applications to areas such as playing strategy games and designing circuits.

The Need for Knowledge

A continuing problem with heuristic programs is that they have very limited knowledge of the world—basically limited to a few hundred assertions provided by the programmer. As Lenat explained to writer David Freedman:

> *The learning you get out of each of these programs is really only what you preengineer into them. It's essentially like a spring*

unwinding. The energy in the spring comes from choosing the right starting facts, and it enables the program to learn a little bit. But the energy runs out long before the knowledge you really need to continue kicks in.

Therefore by the mid-1980s Lenat had decided that further development of reasoning programs would require that a large amount of knowledge would have to be obtained, organized, and codified for use in many different applications. The result would be a large "knowledge base"—a huge set of facts that ideally would be comparable to those available to an educated adult. Although this might seem to be a long detour on the path to developing a machine that could learn and do new things, Lenat had concluded that such knowledge was necessary just as it is for humans. After all a child, no matter how bright, must still learn many specific facts in order to function in the world.

Marvin Minsky (see chapter 4, "Simulated Brains") had devised the concept of "frames," or sets of facts about particular objects or situations (such as parts of a car or steps involved in taking an airline flight). Lenat got together with Minsky and Alan Kay (creator of the innovative, object-oriented language Smalltalk) and together they did a literal "back of the envelope calculation" that about 1 million frames would be needed for the new program, which Lenat dubbed Cyc (short for "encyclopedia").

Cyc: An Encyclopedia for Machines

Mapping out and specifying a million frames would be a daunting and expensive task. Fortunately, in 1975 Lenat had met a scientist named Woody Bledsoe. Bledsoe had been impressed with Lenat's ideas. In 1983, Bledsoe became the director for AI projects at the Austin, Texas-based Microelectronics and Computer Technology Corporation (MCC). Bledsoe introduced Lenat to the company's CEO, Admiral Bobby Ray Inman. Inman had had an impressive if controversial career in naval intelligence, the Defense Intelligence Agency, the National Security Agency, and the CIA.

Inman quickly became enthusiastic about Lenat's proposed super knowledge base and agreed to have MCC fund the project even though he gave it only a 2 percent chance of succeeding.

While Inman was betting a lot of money, Lenat was staking his research career. However, Lenat pointed out (as quoted by Shasha and Lazere) that if this project succeeded

> *This would basically enable natural language front-ends and machine learning front-ends to exist on programs. This would enable knowledge sharing among application software, like different expert systems could share rules with one another. It's clear that this would revolutionize the way computing worked. But it had an incredibly small chance of succeeding. It had all these pitfalls—how do you represent time, space, causality, substances, devices, food, intentions, and so on.*

Building Cyc

Cyc's knowledge base consists of individual items (such as a person or place), collections (such as "plants" or "animals"), and functions that can be applied to items to get new results. "Truth functions" determine whether a relationship holds. For example, the "sibling" relation would return a value of true if two individuals were brothers or sisters. Other functions can return members of a set or extract a subcollection from a collection. Special "modal operators" express tricky relationships such as "X knows Y" or "X believes Y" or "X wants Y."

Cyc is coded in a special Lisp-like language called Cycl. (Cyc programmers sometimes refer to themselves as "cyclists.") For example, the following line would ask whether the item "cat" belongs in the collection "animals":

(#$isa #$cat #$Animals)

In addition to such assertions or expressions, Cyc also has rules that specify how items can be logically manipulated. For example:

(#$implies
 (#$and
  (#$isa ?OBJ ?SUBSET)
  (#$genls ?SUBSET ?SUPERSET))
 (#$isa ?OBJ ?SUPERSET))

This rule says that if an object (OBJ) is a member of a collection (subset) and that subset is in turn a member of a larger collection (superset), the object in question is also a member of the superset.

In order to manage a million and more assertions the data is divided into "microtheories." A microtheory is a collection of items and concepts relating to a particular realm of knowledge. Microtheories

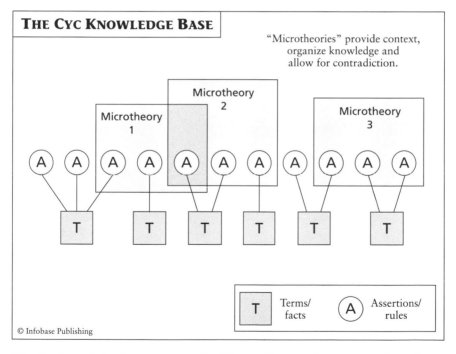

The Cyc knowledge base consists of millions of facts and assertions about them. These in turn are grouped into numerous "microtheories" pertaining to areas of knowledge or aspects of life.

can be related to each other through inheritance. Thus the more general "mathematics" microtheory has more specialized offspring such as geometry. Besides serving as an organizing principle, the other purpose of microtheories is to include rules for dealing with the metaphors and idioms pertaining to a particular field. For example, Lenat points out that the headline "Our Mother of Mercy Slaughters St. Catherine" in a newspaper sports section is not likely to be referring to a mass murder. In other words, microtheories prevent ambiguity by providing the appropriate context for considering a fact.

The actual coding effort for Cyc has a scope unprecedented in AI research. During the period of 1984–1995 when MCC ran the project, Lenat had 30 assistants who encoded detailed knowledge about thousands of everyday activities from shopping to family life to sports.

Today an "open source" version of Cyc is available for public use. Version 1.0 (as of mid-2006) includes hundreds of thousands of terms and about 2 million assertions relating to them. An inference engine, concept browser, and various programming interfaces are also included. The ongoing effort is being managed by a separate Cyc Foundation.

Using Cyc

On the Web site for Lenat's company, Cycorp, which took over the project after it spun off from MCC in 1995, some examples of what Cyc can now do are highlighted:

> Cyc can find the match between a user's query for "pictures of strong, adventurous people" and an image whose caption reads simply "a man climbing a cliff."
>
> Cyc can notice if an annual salary and an hourly salary are inadvertently being added together in a spreadsheet.
>
> Cyc can combine information from multiple databases to guess which physicians in practice together had been classmates in medical school.
>
> When someone searches for "Bolivia" on the Web, Cyc knows not to offer a follow-up question like "Where can I get free Bolivia online?"

Unlike traditional expert systems that use a single inference engine, Cyc has more than 30 separate ones that focus on different types of relationships. Although this can sometimes lead to multiple conflicting results instead of a single guaranteed correct answer, Lenat believes this pragmatic approach is necessary. As quoted by Shasha and Lazere:

We avoided the bottomless pits that we might have fallen into by basically taking an engineering point of view rather than a

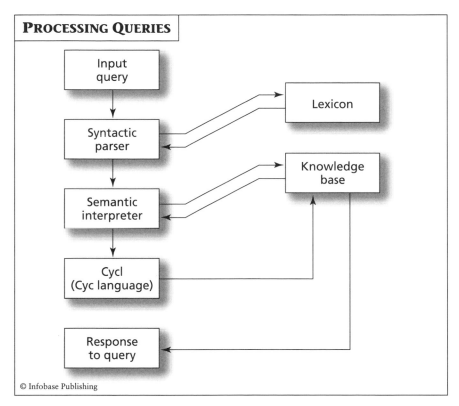

The Cyc system uses a multistep parsing process where the user's query is parsed, interpreted, converted to the special Cyc language, and then matched against the knowledge base in order to obtain an answer.

scientific point of view. Instead of looking for one elegant solution, for example, to represent time and handle all the cases, look instead for a set of solutions, even if all those together just cover the common cases. . . .

It's like you have 30 carpenters arguing about which tool to use and they each have a tool—one has a hammer, one has a screwdriver, etc.

The answer is they're all wrong and they're all right. If you bring them all together, you can get something that will build a house. That's pretty much what we've done here.

Achievements and Criticisms

Cyc is an extremely ambitious effort (it has been called the AI equivalent of the Manhattan nuclear project during World War II). If the project achieves substantial success the results could be spectacular. As in Edward Feigenbaum's speculations about the future (see chapter 5, "A Little Knowledge") a large functioning Cyc system might make knowledge as easy to access and manipulate as ordinary data is today.

CONNECTIONS: MORE USES FOR CYC

The Cycorp Web site lists a number of other applications for Cyc that are currently available, in development, or may be possible in the future:

- Integrating databases that have different structures
- Intelligent Web searching
- Distributed AI systems working across networks
- Online brokering of goods and services
- Improved "data mining" through better semantic understanding
- More accurate natural language processing and machine translation
- "Smarter" user interfaces
- More realistic game characters and virtual-reality displays

On the other hand, some critics in the AI field have viewed Cyc as being overhyped, a mirage that continually recedes into the future. Lenat had originally said the project would take 10 years to complete; around 1994 that was revised to 20. With the project now more than 20 years old, what has truly been accomplished?

On the positive side of the ledger Cyc Corporation points to the growing use of its technology for "bridging" different databases and for intelligent access to information on the Web. For example, through its understanding of concepts used in natural language Cyc could provide for much more accurate retrieval from sources such as the Internet Movie Database (IMDB) or retrieve pictures according to the descriptions in their captions. Ordinary searching relies on matching keywords to descriptions. An ordinary search for "children playing sports" probably would not retrieve a picture captioned "Our first-grade soccer team in action against St. Barnaby's." Cyc, however, knows that first graders are "children," and that soccer is a sport, so it would retrieve that image.

By the early 1990s Lenat was predicting in his article "Programming Artificial Intelligence" (now available in the Scientific American book *Understanding AI*) that with the aid of Cyc technology:

> *Word processors will check content, not just spelling and grammar; if you promise your readers to discuss an issue later in a document but fail to do so, a warning may appear on your screen. Spreadsheets will highlight entries that are technically permissible but violate common sense. Document retrieval programs will understand enough of the content of what they are searching—and of your queries—to find the texts you are looking for regardless of whether they contain the words you specify.*

What is even more startling is that the company also claims that Cyc "is nearing the critical mass required for the reading and assimilation of online texts (news stories, encyclopedia articles, etc.)" This is a very ambitious claim: if it becomes real, then Cyc could, for example, greatly expand its already huge knowledge base by processing the vast and growing Wikipedia online collaborative encyclopedia.

The advantages of Cyc as a resource for user agents (see chapter 7, "At Your Service") might also be tremendous. To function successfully, a program that acts as an agent for a consumer, for example, must know many things about what people consider to be important when buying a house or car. Using Cyc, such an agent could "interview" the user and understand the answers to its questions.

The Cyc Web site claims that

> *the development of Cyc was a very long-term, high-risk gamble that has begun to pay off. . . . Cyc is now a working technology with applications to many real-world business problems. Cyc's vast knowledge base enables it to perform well at tasks that are beyond the capabilities of other software technologies.*

There have been other criticisms of Cyc in the AI community. There are an infinite number of levels of detail for describing any process or activity, and it may not be clear whether the burgeoning knowledge base might become too unwieldy, prone to contradictions or bogged down in details. (Lenat started around 1984 saying that about a million concepts were needed for an effective Cyc system. By 1994, that had grown to 4 million, and later the estimate became 20–40 million.)

How can enough of the myriad "facts of life" be anticipated and coded to avoid Cyc coming to seriously wrong conclusions? Would the size and complexity of the knowledge base that makes Cyc a sort of universal expert system make it applicable to any purpose, but not as efficient as a more specialized and customized program? These questions remain to be answered as Cyc enters its third decade of development.

That said, Cyc continues full steam ahead. Its attractive, interactive Web site (www.cyc.com) offers not only information about the project, but also a trivia game called FACTory. The game is designed to use players' answers to questions to help refine the Cyc knowledge base. The technology remains fascinating, and Lenat's enthusiasm for it seems contagious.

In addition to his work with Cyc, Lenat has promoted knowledge technology widely and effectively. He has consulted with U.S. government agencies on national security-related technology, was a founder of Techknowledge, Inc., and has served on advisory boards at Inference Corporation, Thinking Machines Corporation, TRW, Apple, and other companies.

Lenat has received a number of awards for papers submitted to American Association for Artificial Intelligence conferences and became an AAI Fellow in 1990. He has been a keynote or featured speaker at many conferences.

When asked whether he should have started down the seemingly endless road to Cyc, Lenat has replied: "How many people have in their lives a 2 to 10 percent chance of dramatically affecting the way the world works? When one of those chances comes along, you should take it."

Chronology

1950	Douglas Lenat is born in Philadelphia, Pennsylvania, on September 13
1967	Lenat participates in a science fair and decides on a scientific career
1972	Lenat graduates from the University of Pennsylvania with degrees in math and physics
1976	Lenat gets his Ph.D. from Stanford, having demonstrated his program AM, or Automated Mathematician
1984	Development of Cyc begins
1995	Cyc continues under Lenat's company Cycorp
2004	Cyc enters its third decade with intriguing applications but also criticism in the AI community
2006	Open Cyc 1.0 is released for public use. Cyc Foundation takes over "open source" Cyc development.

Further Reading

Books

Freedman, David H. *Brainmakers: How Scientists Are Moving Beyond Computers to Create a Rival to the Human Brain.* New York: Touchstone, 1994.

Features pioneering AI research of the 1990s, including the Cyc project.

Lenat, Douglas. B., and R. V. Guha. *Building Large Knowledge-Based Systems: Representation and Inference in the Cyc Project.* Reading, Mass.: Addison-Wesley, 1990.

Written about five years into the Cyc project, this book still provides a good introduction to its basic principles.

Scientific American. *Understanding Artificial Intelligence.* New York: Warner Books, 2002.

Includes an article by Douglas Lenat on common sense knowledge and the Cyc project.

Shasha, Dennis, and Cathy Lazere. *Out of Their Minds: The Lives and Discoveries of 15 Great Computer Scientists.* New York: Copernicus, 1995.

Contains a chapter on Douglas Lenat and Cyc.

Articles

"Child's Play." *The Economist (U.S.)* vol. 318, January 12, 1991, pp. 80 ff.

Describes Lenat's work on Cyc and the challenge of making a computer know as much as a child.

Web Sites

Cyc Corporation. Available online. URL: http://www.cyc.com. Accessed on August 16, 2006.

Includes information about Cyc and its applications.

7

AT YOUR SERVICE

PATTIE MAES AND THE NEW BREED OF INTELLIGENT AGENTS

Since the boom in use of the World Wide Web starting in the mid-1990s and the tremendous growth in the volume of e-mail and other electronic communications, the "information explosion" predicted half a century ago has become a reality. The well-connected individual in a modern industrialized state has access to many sources of news and data, and the opportunity to interact with other individuals and businesses using services such as eBay, Craigslist, and MySpace (to name just a few).

The problem is that as good as computers are at storing and organizing data, the technology for extracting relevant and useful information has not kept pace. Search engines are a good example: Many searches can yield hundreds of pages of results, ranked

Pattie Maes has been a pioneer in the development of software agents—programs that can serve as intelligent assistants to help people shop, search the Web, and perform other tasks.

according to some mysterious criteria known only to Google and research specialists. Another example is the vast variety of possible sources for merchandise on eBay and other marketplaces, with varying prices, condition, shipping costs, and other terms.

What today's connected individual needs is an intelligent assistant who can help the user decide what he or she wants and then go online, find it, and communicate it in a form that is easy to understand. Such an "agent" program needs a blend of techniques drawn from data-mining tools, natural language processing, and knowledge-based reasoning. Such practical AI programs are being designed by MIT Media Lab scientist Pattie Maes.

Born on June 1, 1961, in Brussels, Belgium, Maes was interested in science (particularly biology) from an early age. She received bachelor's (1983) and doctoral (1987) degrees in computer science and artificial intelligence from the University of Brussels.

A New Kind of Program

In 1989, Maes moved from Belgium to the Massachusetts Institute of Technology, where she joined the Artificial Intelligence Lab. There she worked with Rodney Brooks, the innovative researcher who had created swarms of simple but intriguing insectlike robots. Two years later she became an associate professor at the MIT Media Lab, famed for innovations in how people perceive and interact with computer technology. There she founded the Software Agents Group to promote the development of a new kind of computer program.

Generally speaking, traditional programming involves directly specifying how the computer is to go about performing a task. The analogy in daily life would be having to take care of all the arrangements for a vacation oneself, such as finding and buying the cheapest airline ticket, booking hotel rooms and tours, and so on. But since their time and expertise are limited, most people have, at least until recently, used the services of a travel agent.

For the agent to be successful, he or she must have both detailed knowledge of the appropriate area of expertise (travel resources and arrangements in this case) and the ability to communicate with the client, asking appropriate questions about preferences (hotel or bed-and-breakfast?), priorities (nature or cultural activities?), and constraints (no sea travel—queasy stomach!). The agent must also be able to maintain relationships and negotiate with a variety of services.

Maes's goal has been to create software agents who think and act much like their human counterparts. To carry out a task using an agent, the user does not have to specify exactly how it is to be done. Rather, the user describes the task, and the software engages in a dialogue with the user to obtain the necessary guidance.

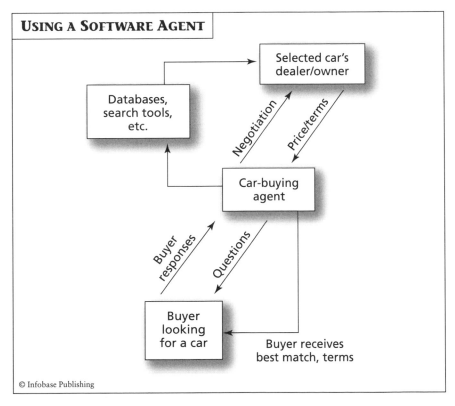

This diagram shows how a car buyer might interact with a software agent. The agent searches for a suitable vehicle and may even negotiate with the owner on behalf of the client.

SOLVING PROBLEMS: HOW AGENT PROGRAMS WORK

Software agents are often confused with expert systems such as those developed by Edward Feigenbaum or programs using the "frames" approach to reasoning pioneered by Marvin Minsky. However, Maes explained in an interview with *Red Herring* magazine that "Rather than the heavily knowledge-programmed approach of strong AI proponents like Marvin Minsky, I decided to see how far simpler methods of statistically based machine learning would go."

The expert system calls upon a "knowledge base" of facts and rules. It generally uses a rather rigid procedure to match rules and facts to draw conclusions. Software agents also have a knowledge base of facts and relationships relevant to their task. For example, a virtual travel agent would understand that a trip may involve several connecting flights, that hotel accommodations can sometimes be purchased as part of a bargain package, and so on.

Part of the difference between the two types of software is in how they use their knowledge base. Expert systems act more like Mr. Spock on *Star Trek,* looking for the absolute logic in every situation. Software agents, on the other hand, act more like people: They have goals and agendas, they pursue them by trying various techniques that seem likely to work, and they are willing to act on probability and accept "good enough" rather than perfect results if necessary.

Expert systems do most of their work on the "back end." They receive facts (such as a list of symptoms), consult their knowledge base, and output the result (such as a diagnosis with various probabilities). For agents, the "front end" of communication with the user is often as important as the knowledge base. Because the user's needs may be more complex and varied, the agent needs more capability to understand what the user really wants or (as a fallback) is willing to accept. The best agents can learn from previous interactions with the user and take his or her preferences into account.

After determining the user's needs, today's agents generally access databases (such as for airlines) or search the Internet for goods and services. In the future agents will increasingly communicate with other agents to negotiate for services.

Today many people obtain their airline tickets and other travel arrangements via Web sites such as Expedia or Travelocity. While these sites can be convenient and helpful for bargain-hunters, they leave most of the overall trip planning to the user. With a software travel agent using the technology that Maes is developing, the program could do much more. It would know—or ask the user about—such things as how much they want to spend and whether they prefer sites involving nature, history, or adventure. The program might even know that a user's daughter has severe asthma and thus all hotels should be within half an hour of a hospital.

The software agent would use its database and procedures to put together an itinerary based on each user's particular needs and desires. It would not only know where to find the best fares and

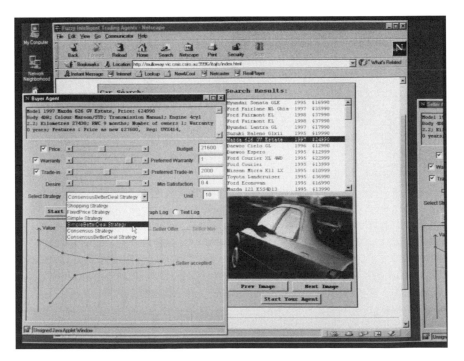

This agent-based program helps users search for, browse, and select vehicles.
(Photo Researchers)

rates, but also it would know how to negotiate with hotels and other services. Indeed, it might negotiate with *their* software agents.

Commercial Applications

In 1995, Maes cofounded Firefly Networks, a company that attempted to create commercial applications for software agent technology. Although Microsoft bought the company in 1998, one of its ideas, "collaborative filtering," can be experienced by visitors to sites such as Amazon.com. Users in effect are given an agent whose job it is to provide recommendations for books and other media. The recommendations are based upon observing not only what items the user has already purchased, but also what else has been bought by people who bought those same items. More advanced agents can also tap into feedback resources such as user book reviews on Amazon or auction feedback on eBay.

Maes also developed programs that, while not involving software agents, used some of the same technology. For example, she started a new venture called Open Ratings in 1999. Its software evaluates and predicts the performance of a company's supply chain (the companies it relies upon for obtaining goods and services), which in turn helps the company plan for future deliveries and perhaps change suppliers if necessary. Since then Maes has founded or participated in several other ventures related to e-commerce. She also serves as a principal investigator in the e-markets special-interest group at the MIT Media Lab. The purpose of the group is to identify trends in electronic commerce, conceive and design new electronic marketplaces, and build tools to make them possible.

Future Agents

A listing of Maes's current research projects at MIT conveys many aspects of and possible applications for software agents. These include the combining of agents with interactive virtual reality, using agent technology to create characters for interactive storytelling, the use of agents to match people with the news and other information they are most likely to be interested in, an agent that could be sent into an online market to buy or sell goods, and even a "Yenta" agent that would introduce people who are most likely to make a good match.

Other ideas on the drawing board include creating agents that get feedback from their user over time and adapt their procedures accordingly. For example, an agent can learn from what news items the user does *not* look at, and use that information to predict how the user will respond in the future. Some of the applications most likely to arrive soon include agent-based Web search engines and intelligent e-mail filtering programs that can fish the messages most likely to be of interest or importance out of the sea of spam and routine correspondence.

Maes and four associates hold a patent for "A Wireless System of Interaction between a Human Participant and Autonomous Semi-Intelligent Characters in a 3-D Virtual Environment." Using such an environment a person can, for example, engage in a deeply immersive 3-D game where the computer-generated characters use agent technology to pursue their own agendas in a humanlike way.

Turning "Things" into Agents?

Recently, Maes has written an article for *Interactions* of the Association for Computing Machinery that begins with an intriguing idea: "What if everyday objects around us come to life? What if they could sense our presence, our focus of attention, and our actions, and could respond with relevant information, suggestions, and actions?"

As explained in the article, Maes and her colleagues at the Ambient Intelligence research group at the MIT Media Laboratory are trying to create such "attentive objects." She suggests that someday it may be possible for

the book you are holding to tell you what passages you may be particularly interested in, while the bookshelf in the room might show you which books are similar to the one in your hands, and the picture of your grandmother on the wall keeps you abreast of how she is doing when you glance up at it.

A number of interesting "augmented objects" have been built at the Media Lab. For example, the moving portrait project has developed a portrait (in a standard picture frame) that has visual and ultrasonic sensors that can keep track of the viewer's presence, distance, and body movements. The portrait can react to this by showing different facial expressions and behavior, being "outgoing" or "shy," for example, depending on how close or agitated the viewer appears to be.

Maes sees a number of reasons for creating attentive objects. Doing so could make the vast virtual world of the Internet and its resources more accessible to the ordinary activities of daily life, many of which do not involve a computer in the conventional sense. Maes does recognize that a flood of information of dubious relevance could overwhelm the user, and thus the information offered by the objects must be personalized and tailored to the individual's needs and preferences. In other words, objects must become capable yet sensitive agents.

Like neural networks and expert systems, agents belong to the "practical" side of AI. However, this does not mean that they are not useful in the decades-long quest to capture and model the essence of intelligence. Indeed, if such theories as the multilayered robot architecture of Rodney Brooks and the multiple agents in Marvin Minsky's "Society of Mind" (see chapter 4, "Simulated Brains") are valid, developing cooperative systems of software agents may be a good way to create an emergent intelligence.

"What Would They Think?"

The technologies developed in order to create better, more accurate agents can also be applied to other types of applications. For example, a 2004 paper by Hugo Liu and Pattie Maes titled "What Would They Think?" presents a model of human attitudes and then applies it to analyzing the likely attitudes and opinions of a person based on his or her available writings (such as weblogs and e-mails).

The model is based on "affective memory"—the fact that the strength and influence of human memory often depends on the kind and degree of emotion attached to the original experience.

Hold requests: 0
Ready for pickup: 0

Thank you for using the bibliotheca
SelfCheck System.

Spanish River Library

Items that you checked out

Title: Artificial intelligence : mirrors for the
    mind / Harry Henderson.
ID: 3365603950594
Due: Tuesday, September 25, 2018

Total items: 1
Account balance: $0.40
8/28/2018 3:17 PM
Checked out: 1
Overdue: 0
Hold requests: 2
Ready for pickup: 0

Thank you for using the bibliotheca
SelfCheck System.

OTHER SCIENTISTS: STACY MARSELLA, DAVID PYNADATH, AND PSYCHSIM

At the University of Southern California's Information Sciences Institute agent technology is being taken to a new level. Stacy Marsella, project leader in an innovative software agent development center, has designed a system called PsychSim. Unlike the more usual kind of agent that has limited tasks and goals (such as retrieving information), Marsella's agents are endowed with simulated psyches. They not only reason their way to conclusions in order to pursue goals, but also they form beliefs about other agents and respond according to those beliefs. PsychSim agents even have a sense of "self."

Currently PsychSim agents are being used in a variety of simulations, including a military training exercise that helps officers learn how to gain the cooperation of officials in an Iraqi village. Another simulation features a "virtual counselor" that helps parents of childhood cancer patients.

The virtual mind of a PsychSim agent includes not only a model of the agent's own mind but representations of other agents the agent has encountered. Thus an agent can try to figure out what another agent might be thinking about him or her and act on that belief. According to Psychsim's cocreator David Pynadath, much of the programming for PsychSim was developed by applying physical simulation techniques (used, for example, to drive Mars rovers) to simulating social interactions. This work, like that of robot designers Rodney Brooks and Cynthia Breazeal at MIT, reflects a growing realization among AI researchers that robots and virtual agents need not only a model of cognition or thinking, but also a psychodynamic model that includes drives and emotions.

Currently much of this research is being funded by the military to develop more realistic training simulations for a variety of settings ranging from Iraq to interagency communication back at home. However, simpler versions of "virtual psyches" can already be found in the Sims computer games and are likely to appear in a variety of online game worlds in the next few years.

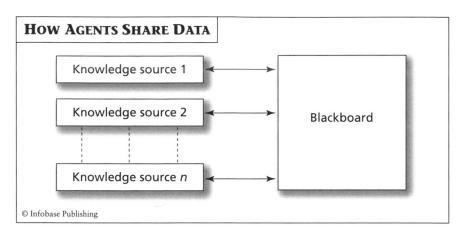

"Blackboard architecture" provides a common area that different knowledge sources (such as cooperating agents) can use to notify one another or exchange data.

Repeated exposures to a person or situation tend to create "reflexive memory" and strong associations between the person and various good or bad qualities.

By modeling these types of memory and "mining" and inputting opinions or characterizations from a person's texts, a model of that person's attitudes can be created. The user of a program based on this approach obtains the writings of people whose opinions are considered relevant, and the system then creates "digital personas" that model the writers' likely attitudes and opinions. In turn, a panel of these digital personas can react in real time to what the user is typing. This system could be used, for example, in getting the prospective audience's reaction to a speech or sales presentation.

Visionary and "Download Diva"

Maes has participated in many high-profile conferences such as AAAI (American Association for Artificial Intelligence) and ACM SIGGRAPH and her work has been featured in numerous magazine articles. She was one of 16 modern "visionaries" chosen to speak at the 50th anniversary of the ACM. She has also been repeatedly

SOCIAL IMPACT: CAN SOFTWARE AGENTS BE HARMFUL?

There never seems to be a new technology that does not bring risks and dangers along with its benefits. The Internet, of course, is a wonderful source of information, but it is also a vector for viruses and human predators. Software agents could also be designed to carry out criminal activities—consider, for example, an agent that knows hacker-style "social engineering" or "phishing" techniques and functions as a sort of virtual "con artist."

Other threats may be more subtle but still troubling. In order to provide desirable personalization, Web sites must record personal and financial information about their users—information that has potential for misuse ranging from sending annoying spam to identity theft. Software agents, to be effective, must be able to find out many intimate details about people's habits and finances, which could be misused in similar ways.

Other critics are concerned that if highly capable software agents take over most of the thinking and planning of peoples' daily lives, people may become passive and even intellectually stunted. Maes acknowledges this danger, quoting Marshall McLuhan's idea that "every automation is amputation." That is, when something is taken over by automation, people "are no longer as good at whatever's been automated or augmented." As an example, she cites the pocket calculator's effect on basic arithmetic skills. However, Maes says that she is trying to emphasize designing software agents that help people more easily cooperate to accomplish complex tasks, not trying to replace human thinking skills.

named by *Upside* magazine as one of the 100 most influential people for development of the Internet and e-commerce. *Time Digital* featured her in a cover story and selected her as a member of its "cyber elite." In 2000, *Newsweek* put her on its list of 100 Americans to be watched for in the future. That same year the Massachusetts Interactive Media Council gave her its Lifetime Achievement Award.

Rather to Maes's amusement a *People* magazine feature also nominated her one of their "50 most beautiful people" for 1997, noting that she had worked as a model at one time and that her striking looks have made her a "download diva." She deprecatingly notes that it's not hard to turn male eyes at MIT because that institution still has a severe shortage of women.

Chronology

1961	Pattie Maes is born on June 1, 1961, in Brussels, Belgium
1983	Maes receives a B.A. in computer science and artificial intelligence from the University of Brussels
1987	Maes receives her doctorate from the University of Brussels
1989	Maes moves to the Massachusetts Institute of Technology and works with Rodney Brooks at the AI Lab
1991	Maes becomes an associate professor at the Media Lab and founds the Software Agents Group
1995	Maes cofounds Firefly Networks
1998	Firefly Networks is sold to Microsoft
1999	Maes starts Open Ratings, software that evaluates business supply chains
2000s	Agentlike programs help users with e-commerce sites such as Amazon and eBay
2004	A paper by Hugo Liu and Pattie Maes suggests a system that can simulate and predict peoples' reactions based on their existing writings

Further Reading

Books

D'Inverno, Mark, and Michael Luck, eds. *Understanding Agent Systems*. New York: Springer Verlag, 2001.
    A collection of introductory papers on software agent design and applications.

Articles

Brockman, John. "Intelligence Augmentation: A Talk with Pattie Maes." Edige/The Third Culture. Available online. URL: http://www.edge.org/3rd_culture/maes. Accessed on August 17, 2006.
  A 1998 interview with Pattie Maes in which she discusses her career and work.
Hendler, James. "Is There an Intelligent Agent in Your Future?" *Nature Web Matters*. Available online. URL: http://www.nature.com/nature/webmatters/agents/agents.html. Accessed on August 17, 2006.
  An introduction to software agents, describing their main characteristics and behavior.
Maes, Pattie. "Attentive Objects: Enriching People's Natural Interaction with Everyday Objects." *Interactions* (Association for Computing Machinery). 4 October 2005, pp. 45–48.
"Pattie Maes on Software Agents: Humanizing the Global Computer." Internet Computing Online. vol. 1, July–August 1997 [Available to subscribers through http://ieeexplore.ieee.org.
  Describes the use of software agents as mediators between users and the complexity of the ever-growing global Internet.
Wertheim, Margaret. "I Think, Therefore I Am—Sorta: The Belief System of a Virtual Mind." *LA Weekly*. Available online. URL: http://www.laweekly.com/general/quark-soup/i-think-therefore-i-am-sorta/8345. Accessed on August 17, 2006.
  A fascinating look at the virtual minds of agents who go beyond simple reasoning to modeling beliefs, drives, and emotions. Such agents are being used in a variety of training simulations.

Web Sites

"Pattie Maes' Home Page." Available online. URL: http://pattie.www.media.mit.edu/people/pattie. Updated January 29, 1998. Accessed August 17, 2006.

ANSWERING ELIZA

JOSEPH WEIZENBAUM AND THE SOCIAL RESPONSIBILITY OF AI

There is something about the quest for artificial intelligence that inspires endless enthusiasm in most researchers. Yes, a given project often turns out to be much harder than had been imagined. When something does work, though—for example, the computer really does seem to understand a spoken questions—there is a thrill something like when a child tells a parent "I did it all by myself!"

There are also criticisms and misgivings about the direction of AI research and its ultimate objective of humanlike intelligence. One researcher, Joseph Weizenbaum, after writing one of the most famous programs in the history of AI, came to become one of the most persistent and cogent critics of the AI project itself.

Weizenbaum was born on January 8, 1923, in Berlin to Jewish parents. In 1934, he enrolled in a Berlin preparatory school, but after two semesters he was dismissed because of recently passed Nazi racial laws. In 1936, the Weizenbaum family, increasingly fearful about the future in Germany, emigrated to the United States.

Working with Computers

In 1941, Weizenbaum enrolled in Wayne State University in Detroit, Michigan. However, the following year he enlisted in the United States Army Air Corps. After the war he resumed his study of mathematics. While working as a research assistant Weizenbaum had the opportunity to help design and build an early digital computer, and although he received his master's degree in mathematics in 1950 he would spend his career in the computer field.

From 1955 to 1963 Weizenbaum worked for General Electric's Computer Development Laboratory as a systems engineer. During this time he would oversee the design and implementation of the first integrated computerized banking system (ERMA), for Bank of America.

In 1963, Weizenbaum returned to academia, joining the faculty at MIT, which had one of the nation's foremost programs in artificial intelligence research. He contributed to the development of the time-sharing computer system at MIT and early computer networks, but the work for which he would be most remembered started with his interest in natural language processing. This was the effort to get computers to communicate in ordinary language and, ideally, to carry on meaningful conversations with human beings.

Joseph Weizenbaum created ELIZA, a program that occasionally fooled people into thinking it was human. However, Weizenbaum became increasingly concerned about the potential for misuse of computer power and AI. (Joseph Weizenbaum)

Ask ELIZA

Trying to decide what project to tackle next, Weizenbaum's career took a turn when Edward Feigenbaum introduced him to Kenneth Colby, a psychiatrist who had been thinking about using computers to develop a new form of psychotherapy. Weizenbaum and Colby then collaborated to create a program called ELIZA, which was

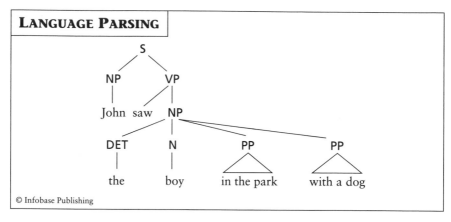

LANGUAGE PARSING

© Infobase Publishing

The first step for natural language processing is parsing, or identifying the grammatical units within the sentence. Here a simple sentence is parsed into its component parts, including noun phrases (NP), verb phrases (VP), and prepositional phrases (PP).

named for the young working-class woman in Bernard Shaw's play who is taught "proper English" by Professor Henry Higgins.

ELIZA has a rather simple structure. The user's input is scanned against lists of keywords, which are ranked according to their likely significance. The program then checks its file of scripts to see if there is one for the keyword. If not, the next keyword is checked, and if none match, a "generic" response is given. However, if a script is found to match a keyword, it is used to generate a new sentence meant to elicit further response from the user. Thus if the user types

I am feeling sad today.
ELIZA keys in on "sad" and then chooses from possible responses in the script, such as:

Did you come to me because you are feeling sad?

ELIZA was remarkable not for its complexity or for innovative use of AI techniques, but for the way it used a few simple procedures to at least temporarily convey the impression that it was a true artificial intelligence—or even, a real person.

ELIZA "mirrored" the user's statements back, much in the manner of the nondirective psychotherapy that Carl Rogers had made popular. A sample snippet of human-ELIZA dialogue might look like this (ELIZA's words are in caps.)

Men are all alike.
IN WHAT WAY?
They're always bugging us about something or other.
CAN YOU THINK OF A SPECIFIC EXAMPLE?
Well, my boyfriend made me come here.
YOUR BOYFRIEND MADE YOU COME HERE
He says I'm depressed much of the time.
I AM SORRY TO HEAR YOU ARE DEPRESSED
It's true. I am unhappy
DO YOU THINK COMING HERE WILL HELP YOU NOT TO
   BE UNHAPPY
I need some help, that much seems certain.
WHAT WOULD IT MEAN TO YOU IF YOU GOT SOME
   HELP
Perhaps I could learn to get along with my mother.
TELL ME MORE ABOUT YOUR FAMILY

ELIZA aroused considerable interest as the first computer program that at least seemed able to carry on a "normal" conversation. In 1966, Kenneth Colby released PARRY, a program that simulated a person with paranoia. The following is a dialogue between a human (playing the role of a psychiatrist) and PARRY:

Why are you in the hospital?
I SHOULDN'T BE HERE.
Who brought you here?
THE POLICE.
What trouble did you have with the police?
COPS DON'T DO THEIR JOB.
What do they do instead?
COPS ARREST THE WRONG PEOPLE.
They arrest the right ones sometimes.
THE LAW SHOULD GET THOSE ITALIAN CROOKS.
Are you Italian?

I Was There: Passing the Turing Test?

In *Machines Who Think* Pamela McCorduck reproduces an account by Daniel Bobrow from the *ACM/SIGART Newsletter* of December 1968 of the experience of a vice president for the computer networking company Bolt Beranek and Newman (BBN):

> *One Saturday morning about 9 A.M., a BBN Vice President in charge of selling our Telecomp commercial service arrived at our PDP-1 computer room hoping to be able to use the computer for a demonstration. He found a note on the PDP-1 teletype that read: "TYPE ALL MESSAGES INTO THIS TELETYPE, AND END THEM WITH A PERIOD."*

This note was left there by one of the programming bums who had just succeeded in making run a Lisp version of the DOCTOR program (based on ELIZA as developed by Weizenbaum). However, the VP thought that this note indicated that this teletype was linked with the one in my home, since I often used the computer all night. Therefore, he started typing to "me," but in fact was typing to this version of the DOCTOR program. The following dialogue ensued:

> *VP Do you think I can use the computer this morning?*
> *TELETYPE Why do you ask?*
> *VP I might be able to make some additional telecomp sales.*
> *TELETYPE Why aren't you sure?*
> *VP My prospective customers have never seen a demonstration of the system.*
> *TELETYPE Does this mean very much to you?*

> *MY BACKGROUND IS BRITISH BUT I WAS BORN IN*
> *   THIS COUNTRY.*
> *Do you know any Italian crooks?*
> *I TRY TO AVOID THE UNDERWORLD.*

PARRY was pretty convincing. In tests, psychiatrists communicating with PARRY over the teletype often could not tell they were talking to a computer rather than a real paranoiac. One reason for

> VP *Of course it does.*
> TELETYPE *You seem very positive about that.*
> VP *This is ridiculous.*
> TELETYPE *Why do you mean this is ridiculous?*
> VP *Is there any reason why I can't use the computer now?*
> TELETYPE *Tell me more about your prospective customers.*
> VP *Please dial me up on 491-1850*

Note that after the last remark the VP did not obey instructions, and left out the period. Therefore, of course, the computer didn't answer him. This so infuriated the VP, who thought I was playing games with him, that he called me up, woke me from a deep sleep, and said:

> VP *Why are you being so snotty to me?*
> BOBBROW *Why do you mean why am I being snotty to you?*

The VP angrily read me the dialog "we" had been having, and couldn't get any response but laughter from me. It took a while to convince him it really was the computer.

DOCTOR (ELIZA) had inadvertently "sort of" passed the test that Alan Turing had posed, in which a human user tries to determine whether he or she is talking to another human being or to a computer. Strictly speaking, though, Turing's test requires that the participant know that one of the unknown speakers is a computer, and the other human. Still, stories like this began to worry Weizenbaum. Would people in the future be regularly and easily fooled by sophisticated computer programs?

this was because paranoid behavior tends to be rather stereotypical, and thus amenable to being scripted on the computer.

The relationship between Weizenbaum and Colby became strained as ELIZA was publicized. Weizenbaum wrote a paper introducing "ELIZA—A Computer Program for the Study of Natural Language Communication between Man and Machine." His interest was, therefore, in how such techniques could be improved and applied in various areas. Colby, on the other hand, described ELIZA in the

Journal of Nervous and Mental Diseases as a possible tool for doing actual psychotherapy. Indeed Colby, with Weizenbaum's help, had created a new version of the program under the name DOCTOR. Weizenbaum, however, felt that Colby had not given him sufficient credit for his work on the program.

Becoming a Critic of Computers

The dispute with Colby over the use of ELIZA/DOCTOR contributed to growing misgivings Weizenbaum felt about the direction of AI by the 1970s. Weizenbaum's 1976 book *Computer Power and Human Reason* marked one of the first attempts of an AI pioneer to address the broader thoughtful public.

The first part of the book sets the computer in the context of human tool use and explains how the power of computation as a universal means of representation and simulation had been discovered. Weizenbaum also gives a sort of introductory tutorial showing what simple computer programs look like and what programmers do. He then goes on to look at the role of the programmer in greater depth. He notes that "the computer programmer is creator of universes for which he alone is responsible. . . . Universes of almost unlimited complexity. . . ." Weizenbaum's chapter "Science and the Compulsive Programmer" is one of the first explorations of the culture of what came to be known as hackers. According to Weizenbaum, the compulsive programmer is like a gambling addict, except that the addiction is to the absolute power the programmer has to control the virtual world inside the machine.

In the chapter "Theories and Models" Weizenbaum begins to discuss the specific theories and agendas underlying AI research. He accepts that the theory that sees humans as "information processors" that can be modeled with computers is not in itself dehumanizing—it depends on whether we avoid acting "as though any single perspective can comprehend the whole man." This is followed by a survey of the work of Allen Newell, Herbert Simon, Marvin Minsky, Edward Feigenbaum, and others who developed models of cognition and psychology—and Weizenbaum and Colby's own experience with ELIZA.

Weizenbaum suggests that by the mid-1970s AI research was essentially stalled, contributing few new developments in either theory or application. In retrospect, Weizenbaum's timing was poor—in the years following the publication of *Computer Power and Human Reason* a whole industry of expert systems would hit the market (see chapter 5, "A Little Knowledge").

A Social Critique

Weizenbaum's arguments about the possible social and moral effects of the technology remain relevant, if controversial. AI researchers had generally been happy simply to ask "what *can* we do?" Weizenbaum, instead, began to ask "what *should* we do?"

Weizenbaum made it clear that he had become dismayed at the ease with which many people responded to ELIZA as though it were human. This posed the possibility that computer technology would be allowed to create shallow substitutes for a human intelligence that science was no longer really trying to understand. Weizenbaum has repeatedly suggested that the only way to prevent this is for computer scientists to take responsibility for their creations. This is the challenge that Weizenbaum believed had not been taken seriously enough.

Weizenbaum believed that computer models cannot capture the rich unconscious life of the human mind or the roots of feelings such as compassion. Thus when Colby talked about refining DOCTOR for use in a clinical setting, Weizenbaum comments that

> *I had thought it essential, as a prerequisite to the very possibility that one person might help another to cope with his emotional problems, that the helper himself participate in the other's experience of those problems, and in large part by way of his own empathetic recognition of them, himself come to understand them.*

Certainly there has been a tradition in psychiatry that sees therapy as taking place through a healing relationship between doctor and client. On the other hand, there is a school that emphasizes mental

TRENDS: "CHATTERBOTS"

Back in the mid-1960s very few people had the opportunity to sit down at a teletype and get online with a computer. It was even rarer to encounter a program that could create something resembling a conversation rather than a menu or command processor.

By the 1990s, however, millions of people were online, connecting to an ever-growing Internet. People were getting used to chatting and text messaging, thanks to services such as AOL and facilities such as the Unix-based IRC (Internet Relay Chat). In this environment many programmers began to amuse themselves by creating their own ELIZA-like programs, which became known as "chatterbots."

ALICE (developed by Richard Wallace) can be thought of as the sophisticated granddaughter of ELIZA. ALICE (Artificial Linguistic Internet Computer Entity) not only has a much more elaborate parser, scripts, and sentence generator, but also she can tell lies or spread gossip told her by other users. The author's attempt to determine how intelligent ALICE was started out in rather promising fashion:

> *Human: Are you intelligent?*
> *ALICE: I am highly intelligent. I have many intellectual functions.*
> *Human: How do you know you are intelligent?*
> *ALICE: By introspection.*

Of course these replies can just reflect a script for dealing with the word "intelligence." More open-ended questions seem to be met by a strategy of "deflection":

> *Human: What were you thinking while you said that?*
> *ALICE: I was minding my own business.*
> *Human: How do you feel about being interrogated in this way?*
> *ALICE: The opposite of not being interrogated in this way.*

Finally, noting that chatterbots often lack much of a capability to retrieve and work with facts, the author tried the following:

> *Human: What day is it today?*
> *ALICE: Ah. It's getting late. Tuesday, April 25, 2006.*
> *Human: What is 9 * 9 * 9 * 9*
> *ALICE: Use a calculator!*
>
> ALICE has repeatedly won the Loebner Contest, a modern version of the Turing test. Her code is "open source" meaning that any programmer can modify or add to her 25,000 templates, which are written in a version of XML, the popular data structuring language.
> One amusing pastime of chatterbot enthusiasts is to put two of the bots into a "conversation" with each other by pasting the output of one program to be the input of another. For example, connecting a rather prosaic "FAQbot" intended to answer questions about products or services to ELIZA is likely to result in an amusing sequence in mutual incomprehension!

problems as coming from cognitive errors—and in that case perhaps some more sophisticated version of ELIZA might be useful.

Ultimately Weizenbaum's book suggests that "since we do not now have ways of making computers wise, we ought not to give computers tasks that demand wisdom."

While sympathetic to Weizenbaum's concerns, writer Pamela McCorduck saw him as having a "curious yearning for a long-gone Eden." Certainly the later chapters of the book are rather in the tone of the early 19th-century Romantics protesting against the burgeoning industrialization of society. Many AI researchers, perhaps not used to thinking in humanistic terms, dismissed most of Weizenbaum's concerns or argued that the gaps he saw between theory and practice in AI were more apparent than real.

Against Oppressive Technology

Weizenbaum's theoretical critique of AI was matched by a social one as well. As the United States plunged into the Vietnam War and racial tension crackled in the streets of major cities, Weizenbaum

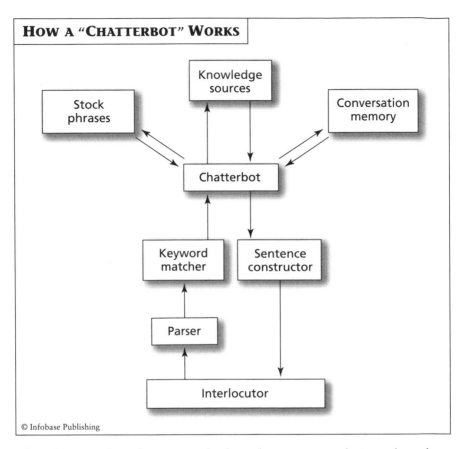

HOW A "CHATTERBOT" WORKS

This schematic shows how a typical "chatterbot" processes the input from the human (interlocutor) and constructs a reply. Note that more sophisticated chatterbots enhance the illusion of true conversation by remembering and returning to previously discussed topics.

became increasingly concerned that technology was being used for warlike and oppressive purposes. Later he recalled that

> *The knowledge of behavior of German academics during the Hitler time weighed on me very heavily. I was born in Germany, I couldn't relax and sit by and watch the university in which I now participated behaving in the same way. I had to become engaged in social and political questions.*

As an activist Weizenbaum campaigned against what he saw as the misuse of technology for military purposes such as missiles and missile defense systems. He was founder of a group called Computer Professionals against the ABM. In a 1986 article he wrote that:

It is a prosaic truth that none of the weapon systems which today threaten murder on a genocidal scale, and whose design, manufacture and sale condemns countless people, especially children, to poverty and starvation, that none of these devices could be developed without the earnest, even enthusiastic cooperation of computer professionals. It cannot go on without us! Without us the arms race, especially the qualitative arms race, could not advance another step.

Although most pundits consider the computer to be a source of revolutionary innovation, Weizenbaum has suggested that it has actually functioned as a conservative force. He gives the example of banking, which he had helped automate in the 1950s. Weizenbaum asks:

Now if it had not been for the computer, if the computer had not been invented, what would the banks have had to do? They might have had to decentralize, or they might have had to regionalize in some way. In other words, it might have been necessary to introduce a social invention, as opposed to the technical invention.

Weizenbaum does not consider himself to be a simple Luddite (like early mill workers who destroyed machinery in protest), however, and he is not without recognition of the potential good that can come from computer technology:

Perhaps the computer, as well as many other of our machines and techniques, can yet be transformed, following our own authentically revolutionary transformation, into instruments to enable us to live harmoniously with nature and with one another. But one prerequisite will first have to be met: there must be another transformation of man. And it must be one that restores a balance between human

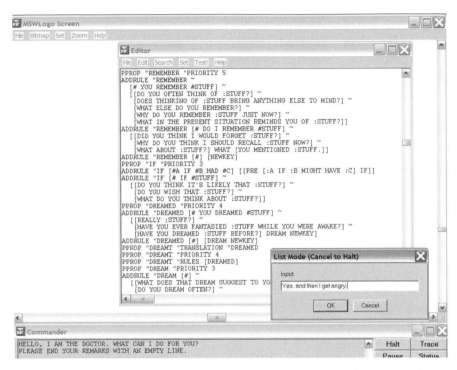

This version of the DOCTOR/ELIZA program is programmed in Java and runs in the user's Web browser.

knowledge, human aspirations, and an appreciation of human dignity such that man may become worthy of living in nature.

As a practical matter, "The goal is to give to the computer those tasks which it can best do and leave to man that which requires (or seems to require) his judgment."

Later Years

During the 1970s and 1980s Weizenbaum not only taught at MIT but also lectured or served as a visiting professor at a number of institutions, including the Center for Advanced Studies in the

Behavioral Sciences at Stanford (1972–1973), Harvard University (1973–1974), and, coming full circle, the Technical University of Berlin and the University of Hamburg. Weizenbaum, along with Hubert Dreyfus, (see chapter 9, "A Philosopher's Challenge), also became something of a fixture at panel discussions debating the pros and cons of AI.

In 1988, Weizenbaum retired from MIT. That same year he received the Norbert Wiener Award for Professional and Social Responsibility from Computer Professionals for Social Responsibility (CPSR). In 1991, he was given the Namur Award of the International Federation for Information Processing. He also received European honors such as the Humboldt Prize from the Alexander von Humboldt Foundation in Germany.

Weizenbaum remains active today as an MIT professor emeritus. Perhaps his best legacy is the growth of courses in computer ethics and the work of organizations such as Computer Professionals for Social Responsibility (CPSR).

Chronology

1923	Edward Weizenbaum is born on January 8 in Berlin
1936	The Weizenbaum family emigrates to the United States to escape Nazi persecution
1941	Weizenbaum enrolls in Wayne State University but then spends World War II in the U.S. Army Air Corps
1950	Weizenbaum gets experience with early digital computers and gets his M.A. in mathematics
1955–1963	Weizenbaum works for General Electric's computer laboratory and oversees the design of the first computerized banking system
1963	Weizenbaum joins the MIT faculty and helps develop time-sharing and early computer networks
	Weizenbaum meets Kenneth Colby and begins to work on natural language programs

1966	Weizenbaum and Colby demonstrate ELIZA, a simulated psychotherapist
	Colby's PARRY program simulates a paranoid person
Late 1960s	The Vietnam War and racial tensions in America spur Weizenbaum to criticize the oppressive use of computer technology
1976	Weizenbaum criticizes AI and its applications in *Computer Power and Human Reason*
1980s	Weizenbaum teaches and lectures about computer ethics
1988	Weizenbaum retires from MIT, wins the Norbert Wiener Award

Further Reading

Books

Weizenbaum, Joseph. *Computer Power and Human Reason: From Judgment to Calculation.* San Francisco, Calif.: W. H. Freeman, 1976.

An introduction to the use of the computer as a tool and a passionate critique of developments in AI and their potential misuse.

Articles

Ben-Aaron, Diana. "Weizenbaum Examines Computers [and] Society." *The Tech* (Massachusetts Institute of Technology), vol. 105, April 9, 1985. Available online. URL: http://the-tech.mit.edu/V105/N16/weisen.16n.html. Accessed on August 17, 2006.

Weizenbaum gives his views on the use of computers in education, the role of the computer scientist, and the influence of military funding.

Web Sites

ELIZA Available online. URL: http://www.manifestation.com/neurotoys/eliza.php3. Accessed on August 17, 2006.

A Java version of ELIZA that runs in the user's Web browser.

"Natural Language Processing." American Association for Artificial Intelligence. Available online. URL: http://www.aaai.org/AITopics/html/natlang.html. Accessed on August 17, 2006.

Includes background on linguistics and computing and natural language parsing, and a section of links to a variety of "chatterbots."

Il Mare Film. "Weizenbaum: Rebel at Work." Available online. URL: http://www.ilmarefilm.org/W_E_1.htm. Accessed on September 24, 2006.

Introduces and provides background for a film by Peter Haas and Silvia Holzinger that presents Joseph Weizenbaum's life and work through his lectures and recollections.

A PHILOSOPHER'S CHALLENGE

HUBERT DREYFUS AND THE ASSUMPTIONS OF AI

Well before the first computers and the beginnings of AI came along in the mid-20th century philosophy had attempted to explain the process of perception and understanding. One tradition, the rationalism represented by such thinkers as Descartes and Kant, took the approach of formalism and attempted to specify rules governing the process. These philosophers argued that essentially the human mind was a machine (albeit a wonderfully complex and versatile one).

The opposing tradition, represented by the 20th-century phenomenologists Wittgenstein, Heidegger, and Merleau-Ponty, took a holistic approach in which physical states, emotions, and experience were intertwined in creating the world that people perceive and relate to.

Philosopher Hubert Dreyfus encountered AI researchers at MIT and became a lifelong critic of the field. Dreyfus believes the model of the mind used in artificial intelligence is fundamentally wrong. (Genevieve Dreyfus)

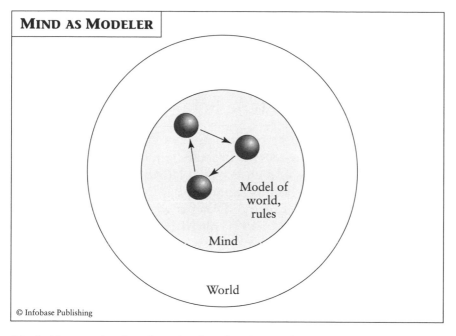

MIND AS MODELER

Model of
world,
rules

Mind

World

© Infobase Publishing

Much AI research is based on the idea that the mind contains a model of the world containing "physical symbols" that can be manipulated by information-processing techniques.

If this is true, no set of rules could be extracted that would be equivalent to the living experience of an embodied individual.

The advent of the computer offered the rationalists a powerful tool. As the AI pioneers began to create programs that acted logically and made decisions, they worked with the assumption that human intelligence could be replicated in a suitably designed program.

Into this milieu came Hubert Dreyfus, born in 1929 in Terre Haute, Indiana. Dreyfus later recalled in his interview with Harry Kreisler that "I was there for 17 years without realizing there was an outside world." Dreyfus claims that his parents were culturally impoverished and did not read books. In high school Dreyfus was interested in science: "I had great fun blowing up things, making bombs, and so forth." Dreyfus wanted to go to the Massachusetts Institute of Technology, but his high school debate coach was impressed with his articulateness and urged that he go to Harvard instead.

The Philosopher and the Robots

At Harvard, Dreyfus majored in physics until he took a philosophy course in order to meet a breadth requirement—and he was hooked. About physics and philosophy, Dreyfus said in the Kreisler interview, "They were both fascinating, but I wanted to understand myself and the world I was in." Dreyfus went on to earn his B.A. in philosophy at Harvard in 1951, his M.A. the following year, and his doctorate in 1964.

As a graduate student Dreyfus taught a survey course in philosophy at MIT. As he recalled to Kreisler:

> *The students were coming over from what was then called the robot lab (it's now called the artificial intelligence laboratory), saying, "Oh, you philosophers, you've never understood understanding and language and perception. You've had 2,000 years and you just keep disagreeing and getting nowhere. But we, with our computers, are making programs that understand, and solve problems, and make plans, and learn languages."*

Dreyfus had specialized in the philosophy of perception (how meaning can be derived from a person's environment) and phenomenology (the understanding of processes). His favorite philosophers, Heidegger and Wittgenstein, said that cognition did not come from a mental representation—a system of "physical symbols" (as Herbert Simon had called them) and rules to manipulate them.

Now Dreyfus was in conflict with the AI researchers who claimed to be developing effective symbolic representations of reasoning. If computers, which at that time had only the most rudimentary "senses" and no emotions, could perceive and understand in the way humans did, then the rules-based approach of the rationalist philosophers would be vindicated.

Against the "Alchemists"

Dreyfus believed, however, that modern philosophy had shown that the rationalist Cartesian view of reality could not work. As he told Kreisler in the interview,

> *Merleau-Ponty says we are an open head turned toward the world. We are directly in a dynamic interaction with the world and other people, we don't have the intermediate of a representation in the mind. And so, I predicted AI was going to fail.*

After Dreyfus had examined the efforts of the MIT AI researchers he went to RAND Corporation and

The history of AI often contains mirrors within mirrors. Here the "Fritz" program creates a virtual representation of a fake 19th-century chess automaton called "The Turk." Now, however, thanks to half a century of programming refinement, this Turk plays killer chess! (Chessbase, Inc., www.chessbase.com)

wrote a paper titled "Alchemy and Artificial Intelligence." The ancient and medieval alchemists claimed to be seeking the "philosopher's stone." According to various accounts the stone could turn anything into gold, make people immortal, or represent a spiritual transformation. Dreyfus's comparison of AI to alchemy was thus provocative in that it suggested that, like the alchemists, the modern AI researchers had met with some initial success in manipulating their materials (such as by teaching computers to perform such intellectual tasks as playing checkers and even proving mathematical theorems) but had ultimately failed to find their philosopher's stone. Dreyfus concluded that the kind of flexible, intuitive, and ultimately robust intelligence that characterizes the human mind could not be matched by any programmed system.

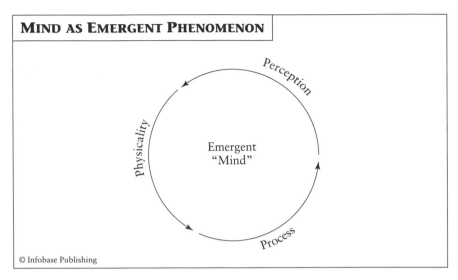

| MIND AS EMERGENT PHENOMENON |

Perception

Physicality

Emergent "Mind"

Process

© Infobase Publishing

To phenomenologists like Hubert Dreyfus, the mind does not contain a model of reality and is not an information-processing device. Rather, mind emerges from an ongoing process of perception and interaction with the physical world.

Dreyfus gave four reasons for the failure of AI. On the biological level, he argued that the brains of living human beings were not really structured like the switches in a computer. On the psychological level, he said that computer scientists have tried to apply ideas from physical information or communications theory (such as the work of Claude Shannon) to the brain, but the brain is the embodiment of physical reality and perception, not an information-processing machine.

Turning to philosophy, Dreyfus said that in terms of epistemology (the theory of knowledge) AI tries to capture what the brain does in a set of rules, but a rule is not the same as the thing it describes. Finally, returning to phenomenology, Dreyfus said that a human has a "fringe consciousness" that encompasses the whole of experience, which can then be focused down into a part as needed, while the computer must painstakingly "count out" a series of discrete steps across a vast landscape of possibilities.

The AI Community Responds

Dreyfus's paper aroused considerable ire in the AI community. In particular, Seymour Papert, a researcher who had worked with Marvin Minsky on neural networks and was developing his own theories of computer-based learning, fired back with an MIT Project MAC memo titled "The Artificial Intelligence of Hubert L. Dreyfus—A Budget of Fallacies." In it he argued first that Dreyfus had a poor understanding of basic programming and computer-design concepts. He also suggested that Dreyfus did not really understand the purpose of the various AI projects he discussed and did not seem to understand that apparent "stagnation" really represented periods when ideas and the computers themselves had to be developed further.

AI researchers also complained that each time they demonstrated the performance of some complex task, Dreyfus examined the performance and concluded that it lacked the essential characteristics of human intelligence—thus claiming that the "philosopher's stone" had continued to elude them.

"What Computers Can't Do"

Dreyfus expanded his paper into the book *What Computers Can't Do*. Meanwhile, critics complained that Dreyfus was moving the goalposts after each play, on the assumption that "if a computer did it, it must not be true intelligence."

An amusing example of this ongoing dispute involves that old favorite of AI researchers, chess. Dreyfus argued that the poor playing ability of early chess programs indicated a lack of progress in AI. However as Pamela McCorduck points out in *Machines Who Think*, early chess programs such as the 1958 effort by Allen Newell, Herbert Simon, and Clifford Shaw were "abandoned" not because the researchers thought that successful computer chess was impossible, but because better programming languages made it much more desirable to write new programs from scratch. At any rate, in 1966 the program MacHack defeated Dreyfus over the chessboard, leading to a headline in the newsletter of the Special Interest Group in

Artificial Intelligence of the Association for Computing Machinery that read:

A Ten-Year-Old Can Beat the Machine—Dreyfus
But the Machine Can Beat Dreyfus

Undeterred by criticism and a certain amount of animosity, two decades later Dreyfus reaffirmed his conclusions in a revised book

---

CONNECTIONS: WHAT ABOUT THE "OTHER" AI?

Although he occasionally mentions neural networks and other "connectionist" AI projects that attempt to create intelligent behavior that emerges from the interaction of many simple components, Dreyfus's critique of AI is focused mainly on "logical" AI—the work of Newell, Simon, McCarthy, and others who use logic, language structures, and other representations to control information processing.

As Dreyfus himself points out, the connectionist or "bottom up" approach does tend to bog down after initial success. It seems that a mass of random electronic "neurons" cannot turn into a high-level brain without already having certain types of structures. Humans, of course, have gotten those built-in structures from hundreds of millions of years of evolution.

However, something similar to evolution can be done with computers. Researchers in artificial life (AL), a field begun in the 1980s, use genetic programming to introduce mutation and natural selection to improve program code.

In another form of "bottom up" AI, researchers such as Rodney Brooks and Cynthia Breazeal have developed robots that are "physically situated" and have layers of components that react to the environment on different levels, feeding information in turn to higher-level components. In theory, such a "situated" or "embodied" AI might achieve human-level intelligence in a way similar to what phenomenologists like Dreyfus claim is impossible to machines that rely on pure logic and information processing.

titled *What Computers Still Can't Do*. While acknowledging that the AI field had become considerably more sophisticated in creating systems of emergent behavior, such as neural networks, Dreyfus concluded that those projects, too, had bogged down.

In talking to Pamela McCorduck, however, Dreyfus made some surprising comments about his decades-long feud with AI. On the one hand he suggested that his misgivings extended to more than just AI:

> *AI is a symptom, and I've generalized it to all the human behavioral sciences. The idea that science and technology can be generalized to everything is something to really worry about and be concerned with—that's my rational reason for what I do.*

On the other hand Dreyfus also admitted that he might have a psychological reason for his attitude as well:

> *But I never asked myself, "Why do I get so upset with people like Papert, Minsky, Newell, and Simon?"—and I really do get upset. It's really puzzling. . . . Maybe, I attack in them what I dislike in myself, an excessive rationality.*

Taking On the Internet

In recent years Dreyfus has found a new technology that he believes is seriously flawed and overinflated in importance: the Internet. In his 2001 book *On the Internet* Dreyfus makes a number of criticisms of the new medium. He suggests that the profusion of hyperlinks and "hypermedia" often makes it harder, not easier, to get a coherent grasp of information.

Because the Internet is virtual and "disembodied," so-called distance learning cannot substitute for physical encounters—this is an echo of his phenomenological and existential critique of the disembodied symbol systems and mental representations of AI. Finally, he suggests that existential theologian Sören Kierkegaard's criticism of irresponsible popular media also applies to the Internet, where everyone can be anonymous in their postings and no one needs to take responsibility.

Experienced users and Internet developers are likely to concede there is some truth in Dreyfus's indictment of the Web, but most would say he goes too far. After all, the Internet is only a generation old, and the Web only a decade or so. Even with millions of dollars invested in new technologies and applications people are only starting to figure out how to use the new medium effectively. (Commercial television, now a bit over half a century old, received many of the same criticisms in its early

---

ISSUES: DIFFERING VIEWS OF COMPUTERS AND HUMANS

In January 1982, a conference was held where several AI luminaries were asked to discuss "the effect of computers on our human self-understanding and on society." A considerable number of religious leaders from the San Francisco Bay Area also participated in workshops after the public discussion.

John McCarthy suggested a cautious approach to the question of whether machines can be self-conscious: "My view .. [is that] one should ascribe mental qualities [to machines] a little at a time." He also suggested that considering the extent to which machines replicate human consciousness may be counterproductive because "human motivational structures are peculiar and it would take special effort to duplicate," given the difference between human chemistry and computer electronics. McCarthy concluded that as for AI, "I think it has a long ways to go. I think there are some fundamental problems that aren't even understood yet."

Joseph Weizenbaum questioned what he saw as a central claim of AI, "that every aspect of human knowledge can be represented in some formal way." He suggested human beings understand things in terms of their experience or personal history. Weizenbaum questioned that such a history could be provided in a string of bits to a computer program. He insisted that "We explain everything to ourselves in terms of something else." In doing so, one finds that "the

years.) Dreyfus's argument that much of the information found online is not trustworthy might be answered by advocates of Wikipedia with its collaborative editorial system—though that is itself controversial.

Still active in philosophy while keeping an eye on the computer world, Dreyfus has had a long and distinguished career at the University of California, Berkeley, where he continues as a professor emeritus. He has won several distinguished teaching awards, was a Fellow of the American Academy of Arts and Sciences in 2001, and was president of the American Philosophical Association, Pacific Division, from 2003 to 2004.

first bases for analogy . . . come from the human being's biological structure . . and needs . . . [Hence] in order to understand the way human beings understand, it is necessary to be a human being." Weizenbaum agreed that computers could still have an effective, non-human intelligence, but there are uses to which such an intelligence should not be put, such as rendering legal verdicts.

Terry Winograd (creator of SHRDLU) stressed a different kind of ethical approach to computers: recognizing the many new capabilities they are making available (particularly in areas such as education and resource management). He asked, "What can be done to try to shape that space of possibilities in a direction that is going to be more beneficial . . . more meaningful and humane? Because the technologies [and applications] will have to be different in who controls them and their costs and benefits, "the development of computer technology (and AI) . . is not the kind of question that you can take a unified moral stand on."

The most radical critic of AI, Hubert Dreyfus, went beyond even Weizenbaum's claims. Dreyfus insisted that "there are aspects of what humans can do which can't be represented [in a computer] precisely because they are not knowledge." Dreyfus also worried that people were starting to believe that only human capabilities that were representable [were important] "put a kind of premium on calculative intelligence . . [Such intelligence] is becoming synonymous with intelligence . . . we are in the process of defining ourselves to be more like computers since we can't get computers to be more like us."

Chronology

1929	Hubert Dreyfus is born in Terre Haute, Indiana
1951	Dreyfus receives his B.A. in philosophy from Harvard. He earns his M.A. the following year
1960–1968	Dreyfus teaches philosophy at MIT
1964	Dreyfus receives his Ph.D. in philosophy from Harvard
1965	Dreyfus publishes the RAND paper "Alchemy and Artificial Intelligence"
1968	Dreyfus moves to the University of California at Berkeley
1972	Dreyfus publishes *What Computers Can't Do*
1992	Dreyfus's expanded critique of AI appears in his book *What Computers Still Can't Do*
2001	Dreyfus takes on the Web with his book *On the Internet*

Further Reading

Books

Dreyfus, Hubert. *On the Internet.* New York: Routledge, 2001.
> Gives several arguments why the Internet is not an effective informational or educational tool, and that it encourages irresponsibility.

———. *What Computers Still Can't Do.* Cambridge, Mass.: MIT Press, 1992.
> Update of the 1972 book *What Computers Can't Do.* Argues that every phase of AI research has failed after a brief flurry of encouraging results, and that the model of cognition and experience used by AI researchers is fundamentally flawed.

Dreyfus, Hubert, and Stuart Dreyfus. *Mind Over Machine: the Power of Human Intuitive Expertise in the Era of the Computer.* Revised ed. New York: Free Press, 1988.
> Describes an "embodied" concept of how people gradually gain mastery of a skill, and argues that computer programs cannot capture true expertise.

Articles

"Computers: Altering the Human Image and Society." *Computers & Society,* vol. 13, Winter 1982, pp. 2–9.

> Transcript of a conference at the University of California with participants including John McCarthy, Joseph Weizenbaum, Terry Winograd, and Hubert Dreyfus.

Kreisler, Harry. "Meaning, Relevance, and the Limits of Technology: Conversation with Hubert L. Dreyfus." Institute of International Studies, UC Berkeley. Available online. URL: http://globetrotter. berkeley.edu/people5/Dreyfus/dreyfus-con0.html. Accessed on April 25, 2006.

> Dreyfus talks about his life, work, the big ideas of philosophy, and their application to AI and technology.

McCarthy, John. "Book Review: Hubert Dreyfus *What Computers Still Can't Do.*" Stanford University, Computer Science Department. Available online. URL: http://www-formal.stanford.edu/jmc/ reviews/dreyfus/dreyfus.htm. Accessed on May 3, 2006.

> Rebuts the arguments in Dreyfus's book *What Computers Still Can't Do* and defends "Logic Based AI."

Papert, Seymour. "The Artificial Intelligence of Hubert L. Dreyfus: A Budget of Fallacies." Massachusetts Institute of Technology (Project MAC), January 1968. Available online. URL: ftp:// publications.ai.mit.edu/ai-publications/pdf/AIM-154.pdf. Accessed on February 20, 2006.

> Papert's harsh critique of Dreyfus suggests that passion and personality played an important part in early AI debates.

WHEN EVERYTHING CHANGES

RAY KURZWEIL AND THE TECHNOLOGICAL SINGULARITY

Because the field of artificial intelligence draws on so many kinds of science and engineering, it has appealed to researchers from a great variety of backgrounds. One of the most unusual figures in today's debate about the future of AI is Ray Kurzweil. Kurzweil began his career as an inspired inventor who brought words to the blind and new kinds of sounds to musicians. Drawing upon his experience with the rapid progress of technology, Kurzweil then wrote a series of books that predicted a coming breakthrough into a world shared by advanced intelligent machines and enhanced human beings.

"I Have Got a Secret"

Kurzweil was born on February 12, 1948, in Queens, New York, to an extremely talented family. Kurzweil's father, Fredric, was a concert pianist and conductor. Kurzweil's mother, Hanna, was an artist, and one of his uncles was an inventor.

Young Kurzweil's life was filled with music and technology. His father taught him to play the piano and introduced him to the works of the great classical composers. Meanwhile, he had also become fascinated by science and gadgets. By the time he was 12, Kurzweil was building his own computer and learning how to program. He soon wrote a statistical program that was so good that IBM distributed it.

When he was 16, Kurzweil programmed his computer to analyze patterns in the music of famous composers and then create original compositions in the same style. His work earned him first prize in the 1964 International Science Fair and a meeting with President Lyndon B. Johnson in the White House. Kurzweil even appeared on the television show *I've Got a Secret*. He played a musical composition on the studio piano. One contestant guessed his secret—that the piece he had played had been composed not by a human musician but by a computer!

Ray Kurzweil's inventions include the flatbed scanner, the reading machine, and the digital music synthesizer. Kurzweil went on to write provocative predictions about how AI, brain scanning, and other technologies will radically transform humanity in a generation or so. (Michael Lutch)

Learning about AI

In 1967, Kurzweil enrolled in the Massachusetts Institute of Technology, majoring in computer science and literature. Because he spent all his spare time hidden away working on his own projects, he became known as "the Phantom" to his classmates. One of these projects was a program that matched high school students to appropriate colleges, using a database of 2 million facts about 3,000 colleges. It applied a set of rules to appropriate facts in order to draw conclusions. This was essentially a knowledge-based expert system, a technique just being developed by the most advanced researchers (see chapter 5, "A Little Knowledge"). The publisher Harcourt Brace paid $100,000 for the program, plus a royalty.

By the time Kurzweil received his B.S. from MIT in 1970 he had met some of the most influential thinkers in artificial intelligence research. In particular he looked to Marvin Minsky as a mentor. Kurzweil had become fascinated with the use of AI to aid and expand human potential. In particular, he focused on pattern recognition, or the ability to classify or recognize patterns such as the letters of the alphabet on a page of text. Pattern recognition was the bridge that might allow computers to recognize and work with objects in the world the same way people do.

The Reading Machine

Early character recognition technology had been limited because it could only match very precise shapes. This meant that such a system could recognize only one or a few character fonts, making it impractical for reading most of the text found in books, newspapers, and magazines. Kurzweil, however, used his knowledge of expert systems and other AI principles to develop a program that could use general rules and relationships to "learn" to recognize just about any kind of text. This program, called Omnifont, would be combined with the flatbed scanner (which Kurzweil invented in 1975) to create a system that could scan text and convert the images into the corresponding character codes, suitable for use with programs such as word processors. This technology would be used in the 1980s and 1990s to convert millions of documents to electronic form. In 1974, Kurzweil established the company Kurzweil Computer Products to develop and market this technology.

Its first application would be both surprising and practical. Kurzweil recalls in his book *The Age of Spiritual Machines* that

> *I happened to sit next to a blind gentleman on a plane flight, and he explained to me that the only real handicap that he experienced was his inability to read ordinary printed material. It was clear that his visual disability imparted no real handicap in either communicating or traveling. So I had found the problem we were*

searching for—we could apply our "omni-font" (any font) OCR technology to overcome this principal handicap of blindness.

Meeting this challenge would involve putting together three new technologies: digital scanning, optical character recognition (OCR), and speech synthesis. Much work had already been done on the first two items, but artificial speech was a different matter. Pronunciation is not simply stringing together a series of sounds. It is not enough simply to recognize and render the 40 or so unique sounds (called phonemes) that make up English speech, because the sound of a given phoneme can be changed by the presence of adjacent phonemes.

Kurzweil's first reading machine was about the size and shape of an office copier. Since it scanned text with a copier-like mechanism, perhaps this was not so surprising. (Kurzweil Technologies)

Kurzweil had to create an expert system with hundreds of rules for properly voicing the words in the text. From 1974 to 1976 Kurzweil worked at the problem while trying to scrounge enough money to keep his company afloat.

In 1976, Kurzweil was able to announce the Kurzweil Reading Machine (KRM). The first models were bulky floor-standing machines the size of an office copier, but they worked. The user was not limited to one font but could place printed material in a variety of type styles on the machine's scanner and have it read in an intelligible voice.

The Universal Instrument

Kurzweil's scanning and character-recognition technology had attracted the attention of the company whose name had become a verb in millions of offices: Xerox. The copier giant was beginning to come to terms with the coming automation of the office and the move from paper documents to computer files. Realizing that there would be a need to get millions of paper documents into digital form, Xerox turned to Kurzweil's OCR software, buying Kurzweil Computer Products for $6 million. With plenty of capital available, Kurzweil looked for an interesting new project. It was not long in coming.

Shortly after its television debut the legendary blind pop musician Stevie Wonder heard about Kurzweil's reading machine and decided he wanted one. Wonder visited Kurzweil, who agreed to provide him with a machine. The problem was that they only had the prototype

---

I WAS THERE: THE OLD ENGINEER'S TRICK

It is a common saying among technical people that there is a "demonstration effect"—that is, a machine's chance of breaking down is directly proportional to how important the people are to whom it will be demonstrated. In *The Age of Spiritual Machines* Kurzweil recalls an example of this variant of "Murphy's Law":

Shortly after the announcement [of the reading machine], I was invited on the Today show, which was a little nerve-racking since we only had one working reading machine. Sure enough, the machine stopped working a couple hours before I was scheduled to go on live national television. Our chief engineer frantically took the machine apart, scattering pieces of electronics and wires across the floor of the [studio] set. Frank Field, who was going to interview me, walked by and asked if everything was okay. "Sure, Frank," I replied. "We're just making a few last-minute adjustments."

Our chief engineer put the reading machine back together, and still it didn't work. Finally, he used a time-honored method of repairing delicate electronic equipment and slammed the reading machine against a table. From that moment, it worked just fine. Its live television debut then proceeded without a hitch.

This educational software from Kurzweil runs on an ordinary PC. It reads documents using a very human-sounding voice and can highlight text as it reads. (Kurzweil Technologies)

they had demonstrated on the TV show. They scrambled to build the first production unit and showed Wonder how to use it. The musician was delighted, and he and Kurzweil became friends.

In 1982, Kurzweil visited Wonder at the latter's new recording studio in Los Angeles, California. They began to talk about musical instruments and computers, sharing an interest that dated from Kurzweil's days as a young "science star." Their discussion focused on the great gap between two ways of making music. Traditional musical instruments such as pianos and guitars produced rich tones from the interaction of wood, steel, and space. Their notes consisted of many overlaid frequencies of sound. The drawback of traditional instruments is that they were limited to a fixed repertoire of notes and only a few ways to combine sounds. They also took a long time to master, so most musicians were limited to only a few "palettes" of sound.

On the other side of the musical world were instruments such as electronic organs and analog synthesizers. These instruments were versatile and their sounds could be manipulated electronically into new forms. Potentially a musician with just keyboard skills, for example, could work with an infinite tonal palette bringing in sounds of horns and strings or even a whole orchestra. The problem was that electronically produced notes sounded, well, electronic— thin and without the rich overtones of naturally produced sounds.

When Wonder asked Kurzweil whether the depth of natural sounds could be combined with the versatility of electronics, the

---

TRENDS: KURZWEIL'S PREDICTIONS FOR 2009

In *The Age of Spiritual Machines* (published in 1999) Ray Kurzweil made predictions about the technology of 2009, 2019, 2029, and finally, 2099. He did this both through narrative and by means of dialogue with "Molly," a fictional character who is portrayed as living through successive technological changes into the indefinite future.

While many of Kurzweil's predictions will not be testable for decades to come, as of 2006 events have advanced about two-thirds of the way from 1999 to 2009. Following are some of Kurzweil's predictions for 2009. Each is paired with a brief assessment of its status as of 2006.

Prediction: Most people use portable computers, which are commonly embedded in clothing and personal accessories. Cables are disappearing in favor of wireless connections. Computers are used for automatic identification and navigation.

Status: Computers have not found their way into clothing, but personal digital assistants (PDAs) and "smart phones" are common. Use of wireless Internet connections is common and in-car and handheld GPS navigation systems are coming into wide use. Radio frequency ID (RFID) chips are also being used but raise privacy concerns.

Prediction: Most text is created through voice input instead of keyboards. User interfaces and "interface agents" respond to voice and natural language and are used for many routine business transactions.

Status: Voice dictation and handwriting recognition are in use for specialized purposes, but most text is still created using a keyboard. Voice interfaces generally understand only very simple statements and can be hard to use.

Prediction: Computer displays built into eyeglasses are in common use. Most computers include cameras and can recognize their owners' faces.

inventor decided it was quite possible. Founding Kurzweil Music Systems, he went to work and released the first Kurzweil synthesizer, the K250, in 1983.

While analog synthesizers had existed for several decades, Kurzweil took a digital approach. His machine was the result of considerable research in digitally capturing and representing the qualities of notes from particular instruments including the

Status: Mostly has not happened yet. However, webcams and cell phone cameras are in widespread use and have had interesting social consequences.

Prediction: Most students learn skills such as reading through the use of "intelligent courseware."

Status: Computers are widely used in schools but not very systematically. Computers have not really changed the structure of most schools.

Prediction: Many new devices are available to help disabled people with daily activities. GPS-based navigation devices help the blind get around. Deaf people can understand speech through "speech to text" translators. People with mobility problems are helped by computer-controlled "walking machines."

Status: Many of these devices are in development but are only in the experimental stage.

Prediction: "Translating telephones" make it easy for English-speaking people to communicate with speakers of other major languages.

Status: Real-time accurate automatic translation remains very difficult to achieve. Online translation services such as Babelfish produce mixed results.

Prediction: Despite a few "corrections," there has been continuous economic expansion due to the dominance of the knowledge economy.

Status: The "dot-crash" of 2000–2002 was more than just a correction. Also unanticipated were the post-9/11 war on terrorism, growing concern about the effects of economic globalism, and the rapidly growing cost of oil. Nevertheless, there are strong areas of growth in information-based industries, including data mining and Internet search engines

"attack," or initial building of sound, the "decay," or decline in the sound, the sustain, and the release (when the note is ended.) The resulting sound was so accurate that professional orchestra conductors and musicians could not distinguish the synthesized sound from that of the real instruments!

Since then the company has introduced ever-improving models of the machine, featuring one that has the capability to digitally "sample" sounds and powerful programming and special effects modules. Kurzweil synthesizers have changed the meaning of "electronic music" for a generation of musicians.

Throughout the 1980s and 1990s Kurzweil applied his boundless inventiveness to a number of other challenges, including speech (voice) recognition. The reverse of voice synthesis, speech recognition involves the identification of phonemes (and thus words) in speech that has been converted into computer sound files. Kurzweil sees a number of powerful technologies being built from voice recognition and synthesis in the coming decade, including telephones that automatically translate speech and devices that can translate spoken words into text in real time for deaf people. He believes that the ability to control computers by voice command, which is currently rather rudimentary, should also be greatly improved. Meanwhile, computers will be embedded in everything from eyeglasses to clothes, and since such computers won't have keyboards, voice input will be used for much of the activities of daily life.

From Entrepreneur to Visionary

As a result of his series of brilliant inventions and new technology companies, by the 1990s Kurzweil had acquired a formidable reputation as an entrepreneur. Sam Williams in *Arguing AI* quotes Ken Linde (chief Web architect for Kurzweil's company):

> *Ray's definitely a can-do guy. He'll sit down in a meeting, explain what he wants, and why it will work according to plan. There's always this positive attitude which, believe it or not, can be a rare thing in the high-tech industry.*

In his 1990 book *The Age of Intelligent Machines* Kurzweil looks back at his career and highlights the crucial importance of timing:

> *Being a high-tech entrepreneur is like being a surfer. You have to ride the wave at exactly the right time. You have to have some idea of where things are going. If your project is going to take three years, you want it to be relevant when it comes out. If it's ahead of its time, it won't be affordable. If it's behind its time, you'll be the 18th person out in the field.*

During the 1990s, though, much of Kurzweil's interest turned from inventing the future to considering and speculating about its likely course. His 1990 book *The Age of Intelligent Machines* offered a popular account of how AI research would change many human activities. In 1999, Kurzweil published *The Age of Spiritual Machines*. It claims that "Before the next century is over, human beings will no longer be the most intelligent or capable type of entity on the planet. Actually, let me take that back. The truth of that last statement depends on how we define *human*." Kurzweil suggests that the distinction between human and computer will vanish, and an intelligence of breathtaking capabilities will emerge from their fusion if a number of perils can be avoided.

Kurzweil's predictions have received considerable publicity as well as criticism. To the extent the future is predicated on the development of "strong" humanlike AI, the critiques of writers such as Joseph Weizenbaum (see chapter 8, "Answering ELIZA") and Hubert Dreyfus (see chapter 9, "A Philosopher's Challenge") are applicable.

The "Technological Singularity"

Kurzweil had already been rather provocative with the title *The Age of Spiritual Machines*. Putting together those two words seems to forthrightly challenge critics, suggesting that there will be machines that not only are as intelligent as humans, but also will embody consciousness, emotion, and all those qualities that are bound up in the tenuous notion of spirituality.

OTHER WRITERS: DAVID BRIN (1950–)

Some modern science fiction writers have tried to imagine the almost unimaginable consequences of fundamental technological breakthroughs such as artificial intelligence, genetic engineering, and nanotechnology. In his article "Singularities and Nightmares" on the Web site KurzweilAI. net, writer David Brin suggests that just as computing went from room-filling mainframes to powerful desktop units, genetic engineering and biotechnology will soon be done with inexpensive, compact machines. But powerful tools also tempt potential abusers. Brin asks:

> But then, won't there also be the biochemical equivalent of "hackers"? What are we going to do when kids all over the world can analyze and synthesize any organic compound, at will?

Brin goes on to note that the danger would be even greater with nanotechnology—the ability to build anything by assembling atoms or molecules. One of the goals of nanotechnology research is to create "assemblers"—tiny machines that can build things, including possibly new copies of themselves. If a "nano-hacker" could build self-reproducing "disassemblers"—machines that can break down structures into their component atoms—then the world might be reduced to what some writers call "black goo."

Kurzweil's latest book *The Singularity Is Near* (2005) ups the ante. The title seems to echo consciously the apocalyptic language of a prophet predicting the last judgment or the coming of a messiah. Kurzweil borrowed the concept of the singularity from science fiction writer Vernor Vinge, who in the early 1990s used it to describe the effects of relentless, ever-increasing technological progress that eventually reaches a sort of "critical mass." In his book Kurzweil elaborates on this idea, emphasizing his belief in "the law of increasing returns"—that not only does technology keep progressing, the rate of progress itself is increasing.

The most familiar example of this idea is Moore's Law, the observation by Intel Corporation founder Gordon Moore that the

Brin suggests that there are a few basic responses humanity might have to the threat of being overwhelmed by technological change. One, advocated by computer scientist Bill Joy, is to renounce voluntarily the development of technologies that are deemed to be too dangerous to pursue. Brin notes, however, that such bans have never worked before and that some government, corporation, or perhaps terrorist group would be likely to pursue the forbidden research in secret.

As an alternative Brin proposes what he calls "reciprocal accountability" —an insistence on open inquiry, vigorous debate, and a thorough exploration of the possible dangers of new technology. Just as advocates of "open source" operating systems argue that having a wide variety of people look at the code fixes errors rapidly, an "open source" approach to these new technologies would make it more likely that problems were anticipated rather than suppressed or pursued in secret.

Whether one takes the conservative approach of renouncing or at least sharply limiting further technological advances, or the liberal one of subjecting them to active scrutiny and public debate, it may be that the singularity itself might contain its own restraint in the form of the only kind of system capable of detecting and rapidly responding to outbreaks of designer viruses or "nano-plagues." Having outstripped human understanding and control, will the post-singularity world be under the care and custody of an artificial intelligence? Brin suggests that human survival might require that such an intelligence be endowed with human values.

computing power of computer processing chips was doubling every 18 months to two years or so. Kurzweil believes that while physical constraints might eventually halt the increase in a particular technology (such as silicon chips) the underlying principle will still hold, and new technologies such as molecular computing, "nanocomputing," or even quantum computing will take over the irresistible march. By mid-century desktop computers will have more connections and raw computing capacity than the human brain.

As he depicts life in 2009, 2019, 2029, and finally 2099, Kurzweil portrays a world in which sophisticated AI personalities become virtually indistinguishable from humans and can serve people as assistants, advisers, and even lovers. Meanwhile, neural implants

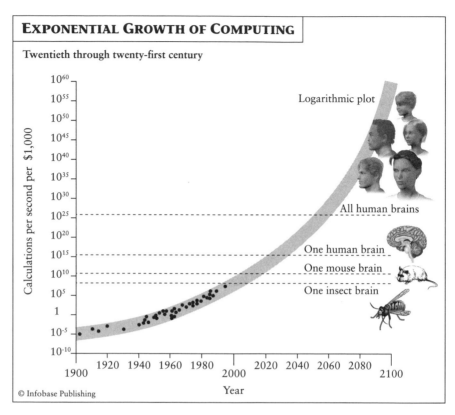

This chart shows the growth of computing power (in calculations per second per $1,000.00) as an exponential curve. Because of the shape of the curve, current insect-level performance is expected by Kurzweil to soar past human levels by the middle of the 21st century.

will remove the obstacles of handicaps such as blindness, deafness, or lack of mobility. Other implants will greatly enhance human memory, allow for the instant download of knowledge, and function as "natural" extensions to the brain.

Meanwhile, increasingly high resolution scans of the brain will unlock the detailed structures and connections of its neurons. This will allow for the construction of more humanlike artificial intelligences and ultimately the "backing up" of complete human personalities or their transference into genetically engineered, wholly artificial, or even virtual "bodies." By taking proper precautions, people will become for all practical purposes immortal. At the end of this process Kurzweil sees a vision worthy of a Gnostic mystic: an entire universe consisting of awakened intelligence.

"Live Long Enough to Live Forever"

Kurzweil continues to engage in provocative projects. Under the slogan "live long enough to live forever," he is researching and

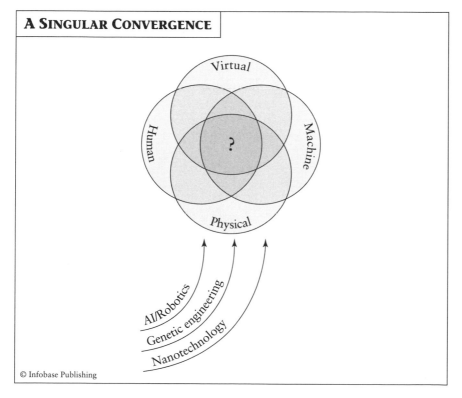

A schematic of the technological singularity. As capabilities in AI, robotics, genetic engineering, and nanotechnology soar, the human and machine merge, as do the virtual and the physical.

ISSUES: KURZWEIL AND THE AI CRITICS

Some critics such as philosophers Hubert Dreyfus (see chapter 9, "A Philosopher's Challenge to AI") and John Searle believe (in different ways) that there are qualities in human intelligence that have nothing to do with computing or information processing and thus cannot be duplicated by any number of computer logic elements or by any software program.

Kurzweil's reply to such criticism is to argue that given a high enough resolution brain scan and enough computing power, the human brain can be functionally duplicated. (Even if physicist Roger Penrose is correct and the brain has structures that allow for quantum computing, there is no reason to assume that electronic quantum computers cannot duplicate even that level of functionality). Thus, since humans are assumed to be intelligent, any artificial simulation of this sort will also be intelligent.

Philosopher John Searle has suggested that even a very complex computer program has no real "understanding" or consciousness of self, and thus can never have the inner experience that people can. Searle used a famous parable called the Chinese Room to make this point. This is a room in which a man who knows no Chinese sits. Questions in Chinese are written on slips of paper and handed through

marketing various supplements intended to promote longevity, and he reportedly monitors his own diet and bodily functions carefully. After all, he predicts that the average human lifespan will reach 120 years by 2029, so if one can live that long one may be able to survive into the age of brain uploads and artificial and virtual bodies—and be effectively immortal.

Whatever the future brings, Raymond Kurzweil has become one of America's most honored inventors. Among other awards he has been elected to the Computer Industry Hall of Fame (1982) and the National Inventors Hall of Fame (2002). He has received the ACM Grace Murray Hopper Award (1978), Inventor of the Year Award (1988), the Louis Braille Award (1991) the National Medal of Technology (1999), and the MIT Lemelson Prize (2001).

the door. By following a series of elaborate rules, the man is able to match symbols in various ways to produce the appropriate answer in Chinese, even though he does not understand what it says. Searle argued that the computer is like that man. No matter how intricate the system of rules, neither the man nor the computer understands what is going on.

Kurzweil and many other AI researchers have countered this argument by saying that it is the room or the computer as a whole that can be said to "understand" Chinese. The man is just a part of the system, just as a CPU is just part of a computer and a neuron is just part of a brain.

Further, in the Scientific American book Understanding AI *Kurzweil argues that*

> *No objective test can absolutely determine consciousness. We cannot objectively measure subjective experience (this has to do with the very nature of the concepts "objective" and "subjective"). We can measure only correlates of it, such as behavior. The new entities will appear to be conscious, and whether or not they actually are will not affect their behavior. Just as we debate today the consciousness of nonhuman entities such as animals, we will surely debate the potential consciousness of nonbiological intelligent entities. From a practical perspective, we will accept their claims. They'll get mad if we don't.*

Chronology

1948	Ray Kurzweil is born on February 12 in Queens, New York
1960s	Early in the decade the teenaged Kurzweil programs his first computer to compose music and appears on the TV show *I've Got a Secret*
1968	Kurzweil develops an expert system to match students with colleges and creates and sells it to a publisher for $100,000
1970	Kurzweil earns a B.Sc. in computer science and literature from the Massachusetts Institute of Technology
1974	Kurzweil founds Kurzweil Computer Products to market text scanning and processing technology

1975	Kurzweil invents the flatbed scanner
1976	The Kurzweil Reading Machine is announced and demonstrated on television
1982	A visit with musician Stevie Wonder prompts Kurzweil to work on a music synthesizer
1983	Kurzweil's first synthesizer, the K250, is released
1990	Kurzweil publishes *The Age of Intelligent Machines,* predicting the future course of AI
1999	Kurzweil predicts breakthrough in AI in his book *The Age of Spiritual Machines*
2002	Kurzweil is inducted into the National Inventors Hall of Fame
2005	Kurzweil proclaims a coming technological singularity in *The Singularity Is Near*
2040s	According to Kurzweil, the "technological singularity" may arrive around this decade

Further Reading

Books

Kurzweil, Raymond. *The Age of Spiritual Machines: When Computers Exceed Human Intelligence.* New York: Putnam, 1999.
> Describes rapid advances expected in AI, nanotechnology, and other fields in the next few decades, as well as the growing symbiotic relationship between humans and machines.

———. *The Singularity Is Near.* New York: Viking, 2005.
> Kurzweil takes on the broader theme of a coming "technological singularity" in which the fundamental nature of human existence will radically change as machines become fully intelligent and enhanced and "virtualized" humans gain effective immortality.

McGibben, Bill. *Enough: Staying Human in an Engineered Age.* New York: Times Books, 2003.
> Warns of the dangers of unrestrained developments in genetic engineering, nanotechnology, and artificial intelligence—and offers strategies for coping.

Richards, Jay, ed. *Are We Spiritual Machines? Ray Kurzweil vs. The Critics of Strong AI.* Seattle, Wash.: Discovery Institute Press, 2002.

> A number of critics, including philosopher John Searle, take on Kurzweil's assertions in his book *The Age of Spiritual Machines,* arguing against the idea that a computer can experience consciousness in the way people do.

Scientific American. *Understanding Artificial Intelligence.* New York: Warner Books, 2002.

> Includes material by and about AI visionaries, including Ray Kurzweil and roboticist Hans Moravec.

Williams, Sam. *Arguing AI: The Battle for Twenty-First Century Science.* New York: AtRandom.com (Random House), 2002.

> Describes the debate over the validity and future of AI from early pioneers such as John McCarthy to the contrasting futures portrayed by Ray Kurzweil, Bill Joy, and Jaron Lanier.

Articles

Joy, Bill. "Why the Future Doesn't Need Us." *Wired Magazine.* vol. 8, April 2000, n.p. Available online. URL: http://www.wirednews.com/wired/archive/8.04/joy.html. Accessed August 23, 2006.

> A noted technologist paints an alarming picture of Kurzweil's singularity, suggesting that out-of-control advances in robotics, genetic engineering, and especially nanotechnology could doom the human race.

Kurzweil, Ray. "The Law of Accelerating Returns." KurzweilAI.net URL: http://www.kurzweilai.net/articles/art0134.html?printable=1. Accessed on August 23, 2006.

> Kurzweil explains the core reason for his belief that true AI and the "technological singularity" will come within a generation or so. Not only is progress proceeding at a breakneck pace, the rate of progress is itself increasing.

"The Muse (Inventor and Futurist Ray Kurzweil)." *Inc,* March 15, 2001, p. 124

> An interview with the entrepreneur turned futurist.

Web Sites

KurzweilAI.net Available online. URL: http://www.kurzweilai.net. Accessed August 23, 2006.

Features discussions and resources relating to Kurzweil's writings and the "technological singularity."

Kurzweil Technologies. Available online. URL: http://www.kurzweiltech. com/ktiflash.html. Accessed on August 23, 2006.

Describes former and current Kurzweil companies in areas such as music, education, and artificial intelligence.

"The Singularity Summit at Stanford." Available online. URL: http:// sss.stanford.edu. Accessed on September 24, 2006.

Provides an overview and materials for a May 2006 meeting where a variety of speakers (including Ray Kurzweil) discussed the "technological singularity."

Vinge, Vernor. "What Is the Singularity?" Available online. URL: http://www.ugcs.caltech.edu/~phoenix/vinge/vinge-sing.html. Accessed on August 23, 2006.

A 1993 article by science fiction writer Vernor Vinge that coined the phrase "technological singularity" and described trends, indications, and possible effects.

CHRONOLOGY

1600s and 1700s	The scientific revolution raises the question of whether humans are elaborate machines
	Philosopher-scientist René Descartes begins his rational inquiry with "I think, therefore I am"
1830s	Charles Babbage designs the Analytical Engine, a general-purpose computer, although it is never built
1854	George Boole publishes a mathematical treatment of the "laws of thought," formulating symbolic logic
1890	Herman Hollerith's punch cards demonstrate the basis of automatic data processing
1914	A. Torres y Quevedo builds a machine that can play chess endgames
1937	Alan Turing demonstrates that a simple "universal machine" can perform any possible calculation
1940–1945	World War II spurs intense development of computer technology, including code-breaking machines and the first general-purpose digital computers
1941	Warren McCulloch and Walter Pitts publish a paper describing the mathematical/logical underpinnings of neurology
1948	Norbert Wiener's book *Cybernetics* describes how machines interact with their environment through feedback
1950	Turing's paper "Computing Machinery and Intelligence" outlines the key issues for future AI research; Turing also proposes a test for true artificial intelligence

	Claude Shannon publishes a paper that describes the basic approach to creating a chess-playing computer program
1952	Arthur Samuel begins to develop a checkers-playing machine that eventually defeats human experts
1956	John McCarthy coins the term "artificial intelligence"
	The seminal Dartmouth Conference brings together the key AI pioneers;
	Newell, Simon, and Shaw demonstrate Logic Theorist, the first true AI program
1957	Many AI projects get under way. Newell, Shaw, and Simon demonstrate the General Problem Solver; McCarthy outlines an advice-taker program
	John McCarthy invents Lisp, a list-processing language that will become a popular tool for AI researchers
	The Advanced Research Projects Agency (ARPA) is established in the Department of Defense; it will fund much computer science and AI research
1958	Herbert Gelernter and Nathan Rochester at IBM describe a geometrical theorem prover that uses a semantic model describing "typical" cases
1960s	Cheaper, more accessible minicomputers fuel AI research at MIT, Stanford, and other centers
1963	MIT student Thomas Evans creates ANALOGY, a program that can solve analogy problems similar to those in IQ tests
1964	D. Bobrow's program STUIDENT demonstrates the ability to "understand" and solve problems expressed in natural language
1965	Joseph Weizenbaum's ELIZA program mimics a psychotherapist and fools some users into thinking it is human
	Hubert Dreyfus's paper "Alchemy and Artificial Intelligence" argues that lack of progress in computer chess suggested that AI itself had gotten stalled

1967	"Knowledge-based" programs such as DENDRAL and MACSYMA use fact assertions and rules to perform tasks in science and math
	Dreyfus is defeated by MacHack, a chess-playing program written by MIT students
1968	Marvin Minsky and Seymour Papert publish *Perceptrons,* suggesting limits to the capabilities of neural networks
1971	Terry Winograd at MIT develops SHRDLU, a program that can manipulate blocks and "explain" its actions
1972	Dreyfus undertakes a broader critique of AI in his book *What Computers Can't Do*
1974	The MYCIN program demonstrates a knowledge-based AI that can perform certain medical diagnoses more accurately than specialists. Desktop computer kits using microprocessors start to appear
1975	Marvin Minsky proposes "frames" as a way of organizing knowledge about the world for use by computers
1976	Joseph Weizenbaum publishes *Computer Power and Human Reason,* suggesting that AI researchers need to take ethical responsibility for the results of their work
	Ray Kurzweil's reading machine puts pattern recognition and sound synthesis to work for the blind
1978	Herbert Simon receives the Nobel Prize in economics. His theory of "bounded rationality" has played an important role in the pragmatic approach to artificial decision making and problem solving
1980	New software tools such as expert system "shells" make it easier for non-specialists to develop AI applications
	John Searle introduces the "Chinese room" parable to suggest that no matter how intelligent the behavior of computers may seem to be, the machine cannot truly understand anything

1981	Daniel Hillis designs the "connection machine," a parallel computer that uses many coordinated processors and provides a new level of power to AI applications
	Japan announces its Fifth Generation project to develop comprehensive AI for industrial and other applications
1982	Allen Newell's team at Carnegie Mellon develops SOAR, a generalized architecture for AI
	The United States announces its Strategic Computing Project
1983	Douglas Lenat begins Cyc, a decades-long project to build a database of human knowledge in computer-understandable form
1985	The "artificial artist" program AARON created by Harold Cohen demonstrates impressive ability to create "original" drawings
1987	Minsky publishes *Society of Mind,* describing multiple intelligent agents within the brain
1990	Ray Kurzweil's *The Age of Intelligent Machines* predicts an exponential increase in machine intelligence—and that a human chess champion will be defeated by a computer within eight years
Mid-1990s	Rodney Brooks applies a "bottom-up" layered approach to AI in creating Cog, a robot with certain humanlike behaviors
1997	IBM's Deep Blue defeats world chess champion Garry Kasparaov
Late-1990s	"Intelligent agents" based on the work of Pattie Maes and other researchers are developed for commercial Web-based applications
2000s	"Smart toys" and household robots begin to enter the marketplace
	Building on Brooks's work, Cynthia Breazeal develops Kismet, a robot with an "emotional model" and sophisticated facial expressions

AI research bears fruit in the form of navigation systems, voice-activated computer interfaces, and sophisticated forms of data mining and pattern recognition

2005	Ray Kurzweil's book *The Singularity Is Near* suggests a coming time in which advances in AI, robotics, and nanotechnology will create a world that may no longer be comprehensible to humans

GLOSSARY

AARON An AI program and robot system created by Harold Cohen. The program creates original drawings and paintings based on an expert system and knowledge about artistic styles.

agent A type of program that seeks to carry out goals that help with human activities, such as comparison shopping or scheduling

algorithm A set of specified procedures for carrying out a task. A computer program is essentially an implementation of one or more algorithms

analog Varying continuously rather than in discrete steps. Most natural phenomena are analog. *See also* DIGITAL.

artificial intelligence (AI) The quest to create software or robotic systems that act in ways that most people would consider to require humanlike intelligence

artificial life The simulation of biological behavior (such as genetic inheritance and selection). This is often used to allow desirable behavior to emerge, such as the ability to solve a problem

autonomy The ability of a program to plan and carry out its actions without direct human supervision

blackboard architecture A system in which several different expert systems or agents can each solve part of a problem and "post" its findings for use by the other programs

bottom up An approach to problem solving that identifies simpler problems (or versions of a problem), solves them, and works toward solving the ultimate problem

brain download A possible future ability to store the contents of a human mind in some sort of computer memory, or to transfer such a stored mind back into a physical body. *See also* BRAIN SCAN.

brain scan A process (such as magnetic resonance imaging, or MRI) used to obtain a detailed picture of the structure and neural connections in the brain

brute-force search A search that systematically goes through every possible item (or branch in the tree). It is exhaustive but likely to be slow.

chaining Moving logically from one assertion to another, as in an expert system. Chaining can be either forward or backward (reasoning from the conclusion back to the starting premises.)

Chinese room A thought experiment in which a person who does not understand Chinese follows rote rules to translate Chinese text. It is claimed that computers similarly would lack understanding while carrying out rote tasks.

cognitive science The study of information processing in the living brain and analogous processing by machines. This is an interdisciplinary field that can draw upon neurology, psychology, computer science, and even philosophy

combinatorial explosion A problem (such as finding a chess move) that grows rapidly in complexity because of the exponentially increasing number of possibilities

common sense In AI, the attempt to codify and use the basic knowledge about the world that humans acquire from their education and daily experience

Computationalism An approach to AI that believes high-level AI can be achieved through systems that logically manipulate symbols and otherwise incorporate reasoning and problem solving strategies. *See also* CONNECTIONISM.

Connectionism An approach to AI that focuses on the behavior of networks of large numbers of interconnected simple units. It is believed that intelligent behavior will emerge from sufficiently complex networks that are properly stimulated. *See also* NEURAL NETWORKS.

consciousness Something that humans feel is part of their essence, but very hard to pin down. Elements of consciousness may include self-awareness, perception of being a "subject," of one's experience, and the ability to experience emotions as opposed to simple neural stimulation

cybernetics   A term coined by Norbert Wiener for the study of how machines interact with their environment and can regulate themselves through feedback

Cyc   (short for encyclopedia) A large project developed by Douglas Lenat that aims to codify a comprehensive range of human experience for use by knowledge-based computer programs

decision tree   A system in which each node is a question whose answer determines the subsequent path toward the conclusion.

deduction   Reasoning from the general to a particular (for example: mammals are warm-blooded; cats are mammals; therefore cats are warm-blooded

Deep Blue   An IBM program that defeated world chess champion Garry Kasparov in a match in 1997

depth   The number of levels to be examined in a tree-type search. In chess, for example, the depth is the number of moves (or half moves) to look ahead

digital   Coming in discrete "chunks" that can be represented by numbers, as in a modern computer. *See also* ANALOG.

domain   The area of knowledge defined for an expert system

emergent behavior   Complex, unexpected behavior that arises from a seemingly simple set of rules. An example is the coordinated flight of a flock of birds.

entropy   The tendency of useful energy (or information) to be gradually lost and chaos to increase

expert system   Software that examines a set of rules or assertions in order to draw useful conclusions, such as for diagnosing faults in an engine.

exponential growth   Growth through multiplication (such as doubling) over time. *See also* MOORE'S LAW.

finite state automaton   A structure that can have a limited number of states, each of which can be derived from the previous state, a new input, and a rule. A stoplight is a simple example: the state "yellow" always leads to the state "red."

frame   A way of describing an object and its characteristics for use by an AI system. For example, a "ball" object might have particular properties such as size, weight, the ability to roll or bounce, and so on.

futurist   A researcher or writer who tries to identify possible future developments or trends. For example, some futurists believe that human-level artificial intelligence may arrive by the middle of the 21st century

fuzzy General term for a system that can have partial or intermediate values rather than simply being true or false. Related terms are "fuzzy inference" or "fuzzy logic"

General Problem Solver An early AI program developed by Allen Newell, Herbert Simon, and Clifford Shaw. It used a combination of rules, search, and evaluation functions to measure how close it had come to solving a problem

genetic algorithm A system in which competing programs contain "genes" of computer code that can be recombined or passed on if successful.

heuristic Referring to a procedure that is not guaranteed to solve a problem but often does work. Heuristics can be used to create practical solutions to problems where formal proof is not possible.

horizon problem The inability of an AI program to reach a solution (or find the best move in a game) because it cannot compute far enough ahead.

induction The process by which general conclusions can be drawn from the experience of multiple cases. For example, after seeing only black crows for many years a person might conclude that all crows are black. Unlike deduction, induction can never be absolutely certain.

inference engine The part of an expert system that takes the user's query and attempts to answer it by following the logical connections in the knowledge base

intelligence Broadly speaking, the ability to solve problems or perform tasks through pattern recognition or reasoning, as well as the ability to learn from and adapt to experience

knowledge base A database of facts, descriptions, or rules used by an expert system

knowledge engineer A person who creates knowledge bases for expert systems, usually after extensively interviewing a human expert in the appropriate field

Lisp (LISt Processor) One of the most popular languages used for a variety of AI projects because of its ability to manipulate lists and create powerful functions

Moore's Law The observation that computer power roughly doubles every eighteen months to two years. This has held true since the 1940s and leads some futurists to predict robots with humanlike intelligence will arrive around 2050

nanobot A tiny "molecular machine" that can carry out tasks and possibly reproduce itself. *See also* SELF-REPLICATION.

nanotechnology The ability to manipulate atoms or molecules directly to construct new types of materials or machines

natural language processing Computerized system that attempts to understand normal human language as opposed to the usual highly structured computer languages

neural implant An electronic device directly embedded in and connected to the brain or nervous system. Such devices currently exist only in experimental form

neural network A system in which a grid of processing units (nodes) are arranged similar to neurons in the human brain. Successful nodes are reinforced, creating a learning effect

node A single "leaf" in a tree structure, or a single point of processing (as in a neural network)

optical character recognition (OCR) The process of converting scanned digital images of text characters into the corresponding character codes. OCR systems are used to convert paper documents into a form that can be used by word processors and other programs

parser A system that identifies the parts of a sentence by applying rules of grammar

pattern recognition The comparing and identification of patterns such as those found in text or images. Practical examples include character recognition, speech recognition, and facial recognition. *See also* OPTICAL CHARACTER RECOGNITION, SPEECH RECOGNITION.

Perceptron An early device that modeled the behavior of a layer of neurons in the brain. Such devices demonstrated the ability to recognize characters and shapes and were a forerunner of neural networks. *See also* NEURAL NETWORK.

phenomenology A philosophical approach that (among other things) emphasizes the "organic" nature of perception and consciousness. Phenomenologists have argued that artificial systems lack such "rooted" connection to a physical body and the world, and thus cannot become conscious in the way humans can

production rule   A rule in an expert system that defines what action or conclusion will result from a specified input

Prolog   (PROgramming in LOGic). A language that is widely used for creating expert systems and related AI software

quantum computer   a device in which each "bit" can simultaneously represent many possible states, not just a single 1 or 0. Potentially this offers a staggering increase in the rate of computation

recursion   Defining something in terms of itself, but on a lower or simpler level. Once a simple enough case is reached, it can be solved and the solution can be fed back up the chain until the problem as a whole is solved

robot   An autonomous machine that can perform tasks or otherwise interact with its environment

script   A description of the steps involved in a common human action, for use by an AI program. For example, the steps involved in eating at a restaurant

search   The process of examining and evaluating possibilities (often represented by nodes in a tree)

self-replication   The ability of an entity to make a copy of itself. Giving this ability to machines raises the possibility of uncontrolled reproduction

Society of Mind   A theory developed by Marvin Minsky in which intelligence emerges from the organization and cooperation of many separate "agents" within the mind that each have their own skills or agendas

speech recognition   The ability to automatically extract and identify words from the continuous sound of speech

speech synthesis   The generation of spoken words through the proper combination of phonetic elements

Strong AI   The belief that sufficiently powerful artificial intelligence can achieve humanlike mental states, including emotions and consciousness. *Compare* WEAK AI.

synthesizer   A device that can use stored information and algorithms to generate realistic sound or speech

top down   An approach in which a problem is broken down until a trivial version is reached. That problem is then solved and the answer fed back up the chain. (This process is also called recursion.)

training The process of "teaching" a system by giving it examples from which to generalize

Turing test An exercise suggested by Alan Turing as a way to identify true artificial intelligence. It tests whether a human who has no physical cues can determine whether he or she is communicating with a machine or another human

virtual reality (VR) A highly immersive computer-generated environment that includes graphics, sound, touch feedback, and possibly smell

Weak AI The belief that intelligent human behavior can be modeled or simulated by a machine, without making claims about the machine's consciousness or inner state. *Compare* STRONG AI.

FURTHER RESOURCES

Books

Allman, William F. *Apprentices of Wonder: Inside the Neural Network Revolution.* New York: Bantam Books, 1990.
> Gives a clear account of the development of neural networks and of the ideas behind them.

Coppin, Ben. *Artificial Intelligence Illuminated.* Boston: Jones and Bartlett, 2004.
> Provides overviews and details for different types of AI systems, including searching, problem-solving, genetics/artificial life, and games, learning, and natural language processing. Some basic knowledge of computer science and math is helpful.

Crevier, Daniel. *AI: The Tumultuous History of the Search for Artificial Intelligence.* New York: Basic Books, 1993.
> Describes the key pioneers and programs and their role in the development of AI through the 1980s, with clear explanation of concepts.

Feigenbaum, Edward A., and Julian Feldman, eds. *Computers and Thought.* Cambridge, Mass.: MIT Press, 1963.
> A collection of 20 classic papers by AI pioneers, including Alan Turing, Marvin Minsky, Allen Newell, Herbert A. Simon, and Edward Feigenbaum.

Freedman, David H. *Brainmakers: How Scientists Are Moving Beyond Computers to Create a Rival to the Human Brain.* New York: Touchstone, 1994.
> Describes a number of interesting approaches to designing intelligent behavior into robots and artificial intelligences.

Garreau, Joel. *Radical Evolution: The Promise and Peril of Enhancing Our Minds, Our Bodies—and What It Means to Be Human.* New York: Doubleday, 2004.
> The author includes robotics and artificial intelligence in a set of technologies (also including genetic engineering, information processing, and nanotechnology) that offer the possibility to transform human nature.

Gibilisco, Stan, ed. *The McGraw-Hill Illustrated Encyclopedia of Robotics & Artificial Intelligence.* New York: McGraw-Hill, 1994.
  Includes A to Z entries for concepts, technologies, and brief biographies.
Graubard, Stephen R., ed. *The Artificial Intelligence Debate: False Starts, Real Foundations.* Cambridge, Mass.: MIT Press, 1988.
  Original essays that now serve to sum up the triumphs and failures of many AI efforts in the 1970s and 1980s.
Henderson, Harry. *A to Z of Computer Scientists.* New York: Facts On File, 2003.
  Biographical dictionary presenting the lives of more than a hundred computer scientists and inventors, including workers in AI and related fields.
———. *Encyclopedia of Computer Science and Technology.* New York: Facts On File, 2004.
  Provides useful overviews of many basic concepts of computer science that are helpful in understanding the background of AI research.
Langton, Christopher G., ed. *Artificial Life: An Overview.* Cambridge, Mass.: MIT Press, 1997.
  A collection of not overly technical papers on artificial life, including its relationship to artificial intelligence and applications to biology, software design, and other areas.
Levy, Stephen. *Artificial Life: The Quest for a New Creation.* New York: Pantheon Books, 1992.
  An engaging account of pioneering simulations of living creatures, from simple cellular automata to genetic algorithms that mimic evolution.
McCorduck, Pamela. *Machines Who Think: A Personal Inquiry into the History and Prospects of Artificial Intelligence.* 2nd ed. Natick, Mass.: A. K. Peters, 2004.
  Revised edition of a classic, engaging account of the people and achievements that have shaped the AI field. Includes many quotations from interviews the author conducted with AI pioneers.
Scientific American. *Understanding Artificial Intelligence.* New York: Warner Books, 2002.
  A collection of informative and accessible essays by researchers, including Douglas Lenat and Hans Moravec, as well as a profile of Marvin Minsky.
Warwick, Kevin. *March of the Machines: The Breakthrough in Artificial Intelligence.* Chicago: University of Illinois Press, 1997.
  Warwick suggests that robotics and artificial intelligence have already accomplished far more than most people have realized. More breakthroughs are coming, and people need to find creative ways to respond.
Whitby, Blay. *Artificial Intelligence.* Oxford: Oneworld, 2003.
  A good nontechnical account of the basic concepts and implications of artificial intelligence.

Williams, Sam. *Arguing AI: The Battle for Twenty-first-Century Science.* New York: Random House, 2002.
> A journalist gives a vivid account of the key issues in the history of AI and how they are still being played out today.

Internet Resources

"AI" Dr. Dobb's Portal. Available online. URL: http://www.ddj.com/dept/ai. Accessed on August 23, 2006.
> Includes news and resources about AI software and development.

"AI in the News." American Association for Artificial Intelligence. Available online. URL: http://www.aaai.org/AITopics/html/current.html. Accessed on August 23, 2006.
> Offers links to many current stories on AI research and applications.

"Artificial Intelligence: History, Philosophy and Practice." Tel Aviv University. URL: http://www.tau.ac.il/humanities/philos/ai/links.html. Accessed on August 23, 2006.
> Provides many useful links to the history, philosophy, tools, and applications of artificial intelligence.

Cohen, Harold. "How to Draw Three People in a Botanical Garden." University of California at San Diego. Available online. URL: http://www-crca.ucsd.edu/~hcohen/cohenpdf/how2draw3people.pdf. Accessed on August 23, 2006.
> Describes a little-known but fascinating aspect of AI: the simulation of creative artistry, specifically freehand drawing and painting.

Havel, Ivan M. "Artificial Intelligence and Connectionism: Some Philosophical Implications." Center for Theoretical Study, Charles University, Prague. URL: http://www.cts.cuni.cz/~havel/work/ai-cvut.html. Accessed on August 23, 2006.
> A good survey and exploration on different philosophical approaches to the nature of the mind, and their relation to the effort to create an artificial network from which intelligence might emerge.

Lanier, Jaron. "One-Half of a Manifesto." Edge 74 (September 25, 2000) URL: http://www.edge.org/3rd_culture/lanier/lanier_index.html. Accessed on August 23, 2006.
> In this downloadable video a virtual reality pioneer cautions readers against "cybernetic totalism," or the idea that intelligence and other human characteristics can be reduced to computation.

McCarthy, John. "What Is Artificial Intelligence?" Available online. URL: http://www-formal.stanford.edu/jmc/whatisai/whatisai.html. Accessed on August 23, 2006.
> A concise overview of the field by one of its foremost practitioners.

"A Proposal for the Dartmouth Summer Research Project on Artificial Intelligence." URL: http://www.formal.stanford.edu/jmc/history/dartmouth/dartmouth.html. Accessed on August 23, 2006.

> The classic proposal for the 1956 conference that effectively launched artificial intelligence as an ongoing field of research.

Searle, John R. "Is the Brain a Digital Computer?" URL: http://www.ecs.soton.ac.uk/~harnad/Papers/Py104/searle.comp.html. Accessed on August 23, 2006.

> A leading philosophical critic of AI argues that the mind is not a computer or computer program. It is a specific physical organ and what it does cannot be reduced to computation.

Periodicals

AI and Society
Published by Springer London
Ashbourne House, The Guildway
Old Portsmouth Road
Guildford, Surrey GU3 1LP
United Kingdom
Telephone: 44 1483 7344 33
URL: http://www.springer.com/uk

Focuses on the relationship between computer science, artificial intelligence, social sciences, and the humanities.

AI Magazine
Published by the American Association for Artificial Intelligence
445 Burgess Drive
Suite 100
Menlo Park, CA 94025
Telephone: (650) 328-3123
URL: http://www.aaai.org/Magazine/magazine.php

An excellent professional and general interest publication on artificial intelligence, as well as tutorials and commentary.

Artificial Intelligence Review
Published by Springer Netherlands
P.O. Box 17
3300 AA Dordrecht

The Netherlands
Contains papers and reports on current research in a variety of applications of AI.

IEEE Intelligent Systems
Published by the Institute for Electrical and Electronics Engineers
1730 Massachusetts Avenue, NW
Washington, DC 20036-1992
Telephone: (202) 371-0101
URL: http://www.computer.org/intelligent
A wide-ranging professional and general interest publication on artificial intelligence sponsored by the Institute for Electrical and Electronics Engineers.

Journal of Artificial Intelligence Research
Published by AI Access Foundation
USC Information Sciences Institute
4676 Admiralty Way
Marina Del Rey, CA 90292
URL: http://www.jair.org
An electronic journal on all aspects of AI research.

Minds and Machines
Published by Springer Heidelberg
Haberstrasse 7
69126 Heidelberg
Germany
Telephone: 49 6221 345 0
Affiliated with the Society for Machines and Mentality. Discusses controversial issues in artificial intelligence, cognitive science, and philosophy.

PC AI Magazine
Published by Knowledge Technology, Inc.
P.O. Box 30130
Phoenix, AZ 85046
Telephone: (602) 971-1869
URL: http://www.pcai.com

A general interest magazine with news, product announcements, and tutorials relating to artificial intelligence applications.

Technology Review
Published by the Massachusetts Institute of Technology
One Main Street
7th Floor
Cambridge, MA 02142
Telephone: (617) 475-8000
URL: http://www.technologyreview.com
Published by MIT, home of a premier AI lab and the famous Media Lab; includes many articles on AI-related projects.

Societies and Organizations

American Association for Artificial Intelligence (http://www.aaai.org) 445 Burgess Drive, Menlo Park, CA 94025. Telephone: 415-328-3123

Association for Computational Linguistics (http://www.aclweb.org) 3 Landmark Center, East Stroudsburg, PA 18301 Telephone: (570) 476-8006

Association for Computing Machinery (ACM) (http://www.acm.org) 1515 Broadway, New York, NY 10036 Telephone: (800) 342-6626

Cognitive Science Society (http://www.cognitivesciencesociety.org) 10200 W 44th Avenue, Suite 304, Wheat Ridge, CO 80033-2840 Telephone: (303) 327-7547

Computer Professionals for Social Responsibility (http://www.cpsr.org) P.O. Box 77, Palo Alto, CA 94302 Telephone: (650) 322-3778

Institute for Electrical and Electronics Engineers (IEEE) Computer Society (http://www.computer.org) 1730 Massachusetts Avenue, N.W. Washington, D.C. Telephone: (202) 371-0101

Society for Machines and Mentality (http://cs.hamilton.edu/~sfmm/) Department of Computer Science, Hamilton College, 198 College Hill Road, Clinton, NY 13323

INDEX